NEW MERMAIDS

CHRISTOPHER MARLOWE

DR FAUSTUS

Edited by Roma Gill
Revised and with a new Introduction by Ros King
Professor of English Studies, University of Southampton

Methuen Drama • London

New Mermaids

1 3 5 7 9 10 8 6 4 2

Third edition with new introduction published 2008

Methuen Drama
A & C Black Publishers Limited
36 Soho Square
London W1D 3QY
www.methuendrama.com

ISBN 978 0 7136 7376 0

© 2008 A & C Black Publishers Limited

First New Mermaid edition 1968
© 1968 Ernest Benn Limited

Second edition 1989
© 1989 A & C Black Publishers Limited

A CIP catalogue record for this book is
available from the British Library

This book is produced using paper made from
wood grown in managed, sustainable forests. It is natural,
renewable and recyclable. The logging and manufacturing
processes conform to the environmental regulations
of the country of origin.

Typeset by Country Setting, Kingsdown, Kent CT14 8ES

Printed in the UK by
CPI Cox and Wyman, Reading, Berkshire

CONTENTS

ACKNOWLEDGEMENTS

It has been a great privilege to revise Roma Gill's edition. I am grateful to the General Editors, the staff of A & C Black, and those of the Shakespeare Centre Library, Stratford-upon-Avon, for their assistance with this work. Some sections on pp. xv–xvii first appeared in extended form in 'In lieu of democracy, or how not to lose your head: theatre and the monarchy in Renaissance England' in *Early Modern Tragicomedy*, Raphael Lyne and Subha Mukherji (eds.), Boydell & Brewer, 2007. I am grateful to the publishers for permission to reuse this material.

Roma Gill dedicated her edition to the memory of her mother. I would like to extend that to the memory of my own, Joyce Scowen King.

INTRODUCTION

About the Play

'. . . make me immortal with a kiss'

Dr Faustus is a play about desire: for the best in life, for knowledge, power, material comfort, and influence. Desire drives human development. It is neither good nor bad in itself and is limited only by the imagination, and by society's and the individual's sense of what is ethical. Therein lies the mingled tragedy and farce of this play. Faustus sells his soul for the secrets of nature, only to be fobbed off with explanations, which were already known to be inadequate when Marlowe was writing. He is obsessed with fame, but his achievement as a celebrity magician is less substantial than it was as a scholar. Rather than protecting whole cities from the plague, as he claims to have done previously, he supplies grapes to a pregnant woman out of season, and plays deliriously childish tricks on a horse-courser – the sixteenth century equivalent of a used-car salesman. His culminating wish to have Helen of Troy as his lover is no different in kind from his servant Wagner's desire to see all the village maidens dancing naked. One sparks some of the most celebrated lines in the whole of English poetry encapsulating all the illicit loves and useless wars in history – 'Was this the face that launched a thousand ships?' – the other is a cue for laughter.

Based on a true story which became a best seller throughout Northern Europe in the 1590s, records show that Christopher Marlowe's play was a money-spinner for the Admiral's Men at the Rose Playhouse in London and became one of the most reprinted of all Elizabethan plays. Ninety years later, however, it looked old-fashioned, and was present on the stage only as a pantomime. In the twentieth century, scholarly doubts about the nature of the text – a sense that the great tragic speeches at the beginning and the end were marred by the comic business in the middle – encouraged theatre directors to remake the play, adapting it to draw out current moral, cultural and political concerns. Subsequent critical work has offered explanation as to why we have two very different early printed manifestations of the play (the A-text of 1604, and B-text of 1616). Finally, the macabre black humour of many recent popular films and TV shows makes it easier to appreciate the Elizabethans' love of plays that mix desperate tragedy with comedy and slapstick. Far from being a relic of the morality play tradition, as has often been assumed, this play was popular in its day because it dealt theatrically and vibrantly with the religious and social problems of its time. Its mix of fantastical story and raw human emotion means that it can still do so.

Summary of the Plot

Appealing for our praise, the Chorus states that the play is not concerned with grand tales of love and war, but with the story of humbly born Faustus: helped through University by a relative, Faustus had excelled in theology, but quickly succumbed to magic through pride in his own abilities.

Scene 1 Faustus reviews and rejects the various branches of knowledge. He concludes that only magic can give him power and satisfaction and asks his servant Wagner to summon the necromancers (magicians) Valdes and Cornelius to help him learn the black arts. A Good Angel appears and urges him to abandon this plan; an Evil Angel tells him to continue.

Scene 2 Two scholars enquire after Faustus. Teasing them with word-play on some principles of natural philosophy, Wagner confirms that Faustus is at dinner with the necromancers.

Scene 3 Faustus begins to conjure and a devil (presumably Mephastophilis) appears. Faustus tells him to go and return dressed like a friar. Mephastophilis enters, in a friar's habit. Faustus believes he has summoned him and can make him his servant. Mephastophilis says he came of his own accord and serves Lucifer. Faustus questions him about Lucifer and Hell.

Scene 4 In a comic reflection of the previous scene, Wagner frightens the Clown into serving him.

Scene 5 Faustus knows he will be damned if he continues on this course, and is again visited by the Good and Evil Angels, but he cannot give up. Lucifer has agreed that Mephastophilis may serve Faustus for twenty-four years in return for his soul: Faustus signs a legal contract in his own blood to that effect. Faustus begins to exercise his new-found powers. First he demands a wife; instead, Mephastophilis provides a devil with fireworks. Next he asks for books revealing the secrets of the universe; Mephastophilis gives him just one volume, in which everything appears to be contained.

Scene 6 Robin, an ostler (stable lad) and clown character, has stolen a conjuring book. He brags that his magic can enable Rafe, another clown character, to have sex with the kitchen maid.

Scene 7 Faustus wavers between despair and desire to repent. When he mentions God, Mephastophilis fetches Lucifer and Belzebub. They entertain him with a show of the Seven Deadly Sins.

Scene 8 Faustus and Mephastophilis, having flown over the man-made marvels of Europe, reach Rome where they engage in slapstick sport against the Pope, disrupting his banquet.

Scene 9   Robin and Rafe have stolen a silver goblet from a vintner. They call on Mephastophilis who transforms them all into animals.

Scene 10   Faustus visits the Holy Roman Emperor. Mephastophilis presents a vision representing Alexander the Great and his lover, and puts horns on the head of a disbelieving knight. On their way home, Faustus and Mephastophilis meet a Horse-courser (dealer) who buys Faustus's horse. Faustus plays two magic tricks on him.

Scene 11   Having staged a magic show for the Duke and Duchess of Vanholt, Mephastophilis, at Faustus's command, provides the pregnant Duchess with a bunch of grapes from the other side of the world.

Scene 12   Faustus's students ask to see the world's most beautiful woman and are overjoyed when Helen of Troy appears. But when an Old Man, observing this, urges Faustus to repent, Faustus despairs, renews his pledge to Lucifer and asks for Helen as his lover.

Scene 13   The lease Faustus has signed with Lucifer is almost up: he begs the scholars to pray for him. Alone in his study, he has a vision of Christ's blood but still cannot repent his bargain. The clock strikes twelve and devils appear to carry him away to Hell. The Chorus laments the 'hellish fall' of a 'learned man'.

The Play

The figure of Dr John Faustus is in part the self-fashioned identity of an historical person, the astrologer, physician and magician Georg of Helmstadt, and in part a creation of the war on witchcraft waged by the religious reformer Martin Luther. A mountebank, not a university doctor, Georg was banned from a number of towns but adopted the Latin soubriquet Faustus, or 'fortunate', as a useful trading name for an astrologer. Luther's followers gave Georg the apostolic name John, Philip Melancthon testified that he died, mangled and destitute in Württemburg (a Calvinist stronghold, see Chorus 1.13n; Appendix 13b, 6–8) and Johann Spies, compiler of the German Faustbuch, attacked academic natural philosophers by making Faustus a graduate of Luther's own university of Wittenberg.[1]

The play has excited passionately held contradictory criticism and approaches because the dialogue expresses passionate and contradictory beliefs, and because its staging demands strong, sometimes exotic, and sometimes unpalatable visual effects. It is a play that mixes high tragedy and low comedy in a manner, which breaks traditional rules of literary decorum. Because of this perceived fault, almost all the criticism

---

1 All this put Faustus in the tradition of Simon Magus, a Gnostic and magician, the first heretic, said to have kept an incarnation of Helen of Troy as a mistress. See David Riggs *The World of Christopher Marlowe* (2004) 233–5.

concentrates on the nature of Faustus's pact with the devil and therefore on the great speeches he makes in the first few scenes and at the very end of the play. The comic scenes – not just those between Rafe and Robin, but also the slapstick with Faustus and the Pope or the Horse-courser – have been almost entirely disregarded. Of course humour is often much more difficult to read and appreciate on the page. But we should not forget that despite its printed title (*The Tragical History of Doctor Faustus*), almost everything that we can deduce about its early existence on the stage is that it owed its undoubted popularity to its spectacle and humour. Susan Snyder rather grudgingly recognises this when she remarks that despite its apparent flaws, the play does indeed work 'as spectacle'.[2]

Our impressions as to what Marlowe wrote are dependent on the texts that have come down to us in print. His play *The Jew of Malta* creates an irresistible blend of black humour, violence and tragedy, but *Tamburlaine* may originally have been much funnier than it appears to us now, for the play's printer, Richard Jones, in his address to the reader, claims that he has removed what he regards as extraneous comic material. In fact, the mixed genre is by far the most frequent form in early modern English theatre.[3] Almost all of Shakespeare's plays blend tragic and comic elements. But in the late seventeenth century, with a narrow definition of tragic form derived from Aristotle's prescription for a high style unmingled with comedy or low-life characters, Marlowe's play fell out of fashion as serious drama and was performed at Lincoln's Inn Field in 1697 as a farce, with the pantomime characters of Harlequin and Scaramouche replacing and amplifying the roles of Robin and Rafe (or Dick in the B-text). Later the story was reworked by Johann Wolfgang von Goethe into an immense two part play, originally designed for reading rather than performance. In the words of Howard Brenton's translation for the RSC (1995), it too is a 'show/ About life and death/ Funny and philosophical/ In one breath'.[4] In short, the popularity of both the story and Marlowe's play has always depended on its mix of farce and tragedy, and on a structure which invites topical additions to its comic aspects.

Perhaps the most frequently repeated misapprehension in Marlowe criticism is that *Doctor Faustus* is a relic of the medieval morality play

2 Susan Snyder, '*Doctor Faustus* as an inverted Saint's Life' in *Doctor Faustus*, ed. by David Scott Kastan, 2005, p. 320.

3 The first designated 'tragical comedy' in English was Richard Edwards's entertaining and influential *Damon and Pythias* (1564), see Ros King, *The Works of Richard Edwards*, 2001.

4 Johann Wolfgang von Goethe, *Faust parts 1 and II*, in a new version by Howard Brenton, 1995.

tradition. In plays such as *Everyman* or *Magnifycence*, the central epony-mous character is subject to psychomachia, a battle for his soul by the forces of good and evil. He is tempted, succumbs, sees the error of his ways, repents, and is saved. Faustus, however, willingly gives his soul to the devil, enjoys himself, cannot repent and is damned. In the A-text version of *Doctor Faustus*, Mephastophilis never acts without first being prompted to do so by Faustus, often behaving as a world-weary commen-tator on the action; he is therefore not a medieval Vice figure.

Faustus and Salvation

The changes in religious belief in England during the lifetimes of Marlowe and his parents were more complex than is commonly realised. It is not simply that the official religion of the country broke from the Roman Catholic church in the 1530s under Henry VIII, returned to Catholicism under his daughter Mary I (reigned 1553–1558), and reverted to Protes-tantism with the accession of his younger daughter Elizabeth I (reigned 1558–1603). The English church and its required forms of ritual obser-vance changed profoundly during those same seventy years. Initially adopting the reformed religion of Martin Luther, who believed in justi-fication (salvation) through faith alone, it soon embraced and then gradually discarded John Calvin's more stringent form of Protestantism, which maintained that some people were 'elect' or 'predestined' to be saved after death and others were 'predestined' to be damned. None of these religious changes was clear-cut, however, and the actual nature of belief amongst English people, in so far as that can now be determined, varied enormously, both between individuals and over time.[5]

For most ordinary people, religion consists in 'observance' – the prescribed actions required to show devotion. But if those actions are changed merely at the behest of people in political power, then the validity of religion itself is brought into question. The result may be a growth in 'atheism'. While there has been much debate over the meaning of that word in the sixteenth century, it is likely that there were many who were living 'without god' in one way or another, or were sceptical in their beliefs.[6] The Cambridge divine William Perkins wrote, albeit no doubt with some exaggeration: 'The reprobate for all this knowledge, in his

---

5 See for example, Diarmaid MacCulloch, *Thomas Cranmer: a Life*, 1996, e.g. pp. 173–236; Judith Maltby, *Prayer Book and People in Elizabethan and Early Stuart England*, 1998, pp.1–30.
6 See Richard H. Popkin, *The History of Scepticism from Erasmus to Descartes*, 1964; Michael Hunter and David Wootton (eds.), *Atheism from the Reformation to the Enlightenment*, 1992.

heart may be an Atheist, as David saith: the foole hath saide in his heart there is no God [Psal. xiv, 1; Rom. 3. 10. 11]. And a man may nowe a daies finde houses and townes full of such fooles'.[7]

The University of Cambridge, where Marlowe was enrolled as a student of Divinity from 1580–1587, was a centre for radical Calvinism. Perkins, whose works were much reprinted during and after his lifetime, was attempting a seemingly impossible task of central importance to the Elizabethan church: to reconcile Calvinist predestination with salvation for all who believe in the efficacy of Christ's sacrifice.[8] This argument is worth exploring in detail since it highlights Faustus's logical difficulties concerning salvation. Perkins's approach to the problem was not original and follows the refinements to Calvinism set out half a century earlier by the French Protestant theologian, Theodore Beza. Beza had tried to answer the problem in a handbook aimed at the general reader consisting of simple questions and answers. This had been translated into English in 1572 and reprinted several times.[9] The answers in this little book are generally patient, brief, pithy and clearly written. But when Beza gets to the problem of the elect, they become hugely extended and convoluted: on the one hand, the elect are chosen by God; on the other, the wicked have chosen not to believe in God's mercy, which would otherwise be open to them through Christ's sacrifice.

The solution is faith, which as Perkins puts it, is 'a wonderfull grace of God, by which the Elect doe apprehende and apply Christ and all his benefites unto themselues particularly' (Perkins, 29). God begets faith in his elect. But before he can do so, individuals must acquire knowledge of the bible:

> The manner that God useth in the begetting of faith is this. First he prepareth the heart that it maie be capable of faith. Secondlie he causeth faith by little and little to spring and to breed in the heart. The preparation of the heart is by humbling and softening of it: and to the doing of this there are foure things requisite. The first of them is the knowledge of the word of God, both of the lawe and of the Gospell, without the which there can bee no faith;   (Perkins, 33)

---

7 William Perkins, *A treatise tending vnto a declaration whether a man be in the estate of damnation or in the estate of grace and if he be in the first, how he may in time come out of it: if in the second, how he maie discerne it, and perseuere in the same to the end,* 1590, p. 3.

8 See also G. M. Pinciss, 'Marlowe's Cambridge Years and the Writing of Doctor Faustus', *Studies in English Literature, 1500–1900,* Vol. 33, No. 2, Elizabethan and Jacobean Drama (1993), pp. 249–64.

9 Theodore Beza, *A Booke of Christian Questions and Answers,* tr Arthur Golding, 1572.

But God also begets lack of faith in the reprobate:

> . . . after a certaine time God in his just judgement hardeneth their harts, blindeth the eies of their minds, he maketh their heads giddie with a spirituall drunkennes, and by the strength of their inward lusts, as also by the effectuall operation of Satan, they fall to open infidelitie, and contempt of Gods word, and so runne headlong to their own damnation, and perish finally. (Perkins, 22)

Lack of faith means that the wicked believe 'their sinnes are greater, th[a]n that they can be forgiven' (Perkins, 50).

The behaviour of Marlowe's Faustus seems to follow Perkins's Calvinist theology quite closely. Faustus has extensive knowledge of Christian texts, better than any other divine in Wittenberg, but his heart, as Perkins would say, is 'hardened'. He is proud of his worldly achievements, and he comes to believe that he is beyond redemption. He has no faith.

This apparently orthodox stance, combined with the play's evident antipapal satire, probably enabled it to escape interference from the censors. Yet the play's dramaturgy (its structure, language, and potential for performance) opens up quite other possibilities. The name Faustus was common in the theological works to which Marlowe, as a student of divinity, would have been exposed. Faustus of Milevis, or Faustus the Manichee, is repeatedly cited as an example of extreme wrongheadedness in the writings of another prolific Cambridge divine, William Fulke (1536–89), a popular preacher with extreme opinions, but vice-chancellor of the university during Marlowe's first year as a student. Manichaeism, which combined Gnosticism (salvation through revealed knowledge and reason) and dualism (belief in the equal and opposing forces of good and evil) was known through the writings of St Augustine, who as a young man, had enrolled himself as a follower of this Faustus before exposing him as a fraud in *Contra Faustum Manichaeum*. He found this Faustus eloquent but ignorant, and his religion based on a palpably false cosmology drawn from 'fables' of the sun and moon, rather than the knowledge that Augustine himself had learnt through books of 'secular philosophy' and the evidence of his own eyes (*Confessions*, 5.7.12; 5.3.6).

In this religious context, the Good and Evil Angels are not so much relics of medieval Catholicism as a Manichaean gloss on the Calvinism in the play. Calvin had dismissed the foolish belief of the 'common people' that each individual was assigned a particular pair of good and bad angels, since the whole company of angels defends and serves the company of the godly.[10] Indeed Faustus scarcely seems to hear them, merely picking up occasionally on odd words. Dramaturgically, the equal and opposite assertions of the two angels cancel each other out, but usually leave the Evil Angel with the last word and therefore the upper hand. The Good Angel, ironically, in urging Faustus to 'lay that damned book aside' (1.70) reinforces his sense of the inadequacy of received knowledge, the knowledge that is to be found in books, and his desire instead for revealed knowledge: he wants Mephastophilis to *show* him the truth. The Evil Angel in urging him the way he is going 'Go forward, Faustus, in that famous art/ Wherein all nature's treasury is contained' offers him a glimpse of empirical knowledge as well as a promise of worldly power (1.74–8).

The play thus dramatises a philosophical question: what is the criterion for truth? Books, or perhaps rather the authority of the allowed written word, are very much the problem. Faustus's dissatisfaction with the state of received human knowledge is presented both linguistically and visually in the first scene as he sets aside the tomes that represent the summation of each academic discipline. He knows enough to be dissatisfied by the limitations of rhetorical argument and is desperate for concrete experiential knowledge to cut through the mass of contradictory theories culled from an array of philosophers and traditions. He asks Mephastophilis for the truth about hell and, in what may be a playful reversal of the story of Augustine and Faustus the Manichee, is fobbed off with a 'fable' (5.126). Mephastophilis can do nothing but repeat familiar 'truths', which some in the audience may have known to have been questioned if not refuted by science. Faustus's tacit acceptance of what Mephastophilis tells him, although clearly he knows it to be inadequate, again calls into question the validity of all received knowledge. Mephastophilis, of course, knows about the relationship between knowledge and experience: 'Ay, think so still, till experience change thy mind' (5.127). Having sidestepped Faustus's direct questions, Mephastophilis gives him a book. This is comfortingly familiar territory and in the B-text Faustus is content. In the A-text, Faustus then asks for an additional book that will let him conjure spirits when he pleases. Mephastophilis merely turns the pages of the book he has already supplied. Faustus asks for a book that will show him the movement of the planets. Again, Mephastophilis turns the pages. Now Faustus pleads for 'one book more' detailing all plants and trees. Mephastophilis turns the pages (5.165–174). All of creation in just one book? All already written down? Is it for this

10 Jean Calvin, *The Institution of Christian Religion*, 1561, F6v.

that he has sold his soul? The repetition of demand and page-turning means that the audience anticipates what is coming. It is even blackly humorous. Faustus, however, is dismayed. Given his terrible bargain, his comment 'O, thou art deceived' (5.173) is arguably the most tragic moment in the play.

This, then, is the dramaturgical reason for arguing that what appears in the A-text as a single long scene between Faustus and Mephastophilis is really two scenes: Scenes 5 and 7 in this edition. There is a very real difference in tone. In scene 5, Mephastophilis is still trying to secure Faustus's soul with a legal contract, and Faustus himself still has real scientific and philosophical questions to which he wants answers. In scene 7 (the second half of the A-text's long scene) he is being diverted by theatrical shows. It is only when split into two that the real tragedy of Faustus's choice comes into focus.

The A-text in particular thus presents a situation in which what God and the Devil have to offer in this life are equally unsatisfactory. The Devil provides a dubious account of cosmology, a show of seven pretty un-pleasant and unalluring deadly sins, and a devil with a firework, instead of a wife. God, through the Old Man, on the other hand, offers blood and tears. No wonder Faustus turns to despair. The audience safe in the theatre, observing this story, and enjoying its staging, can observe the problem but is not forced down the same emotional road. Each scene that shows Faustus grasping after demonstrable truth while being deflected with conven-tional *a priori* argument is followed by a scene in which Rafe and Robin reduce that particular aspect of the problem to absurdity. Their comic antics likewise depend on the use of books. For the present argument, it does not matter who wrote these scenes, whether Marlowe or a collabo-rator, only that they work dramaturgically to turn the tragic scenes on their head. Robin's horizons are more limited than Faustus's, but he is just as likely to be disappointed: 'here I ha' stol'n one of Doctor Faustus' conjuring books [. . .] now will I make all the maidens in our parish dance at my pleasure stark naked before me, and so by that means I shall see more than ere I felt or saw yet' (6.1–5). The scene ends bathetically as he goes to clean his boots. The next time he appears, he has forgotten his impossible dream about naked girls, and has turned to petty theft.

It is therefore interesting that once Faustus is in command of his own magic choices (although of course he is entirely dependent on Mephas-tophilis for their execution) the nature of his desires changes. He reports that he has flown round the world, seeing first hand the wonders of the natural world and, no less marvellous, the cities built by man: Trier, Paris, Naples, 'Venice – Padua and the rest' (8.1–19). The shows with which he

Dr Faustus (Eric Porter, seated), Mephastophilis (Terrence Hardiman) and the Seven Deadly Sins. Scene from Clifford Williams's 1968 production for the Royal Shakespeare Company. Copyright Douglas H Jeffery. Image supplied by the Shakespeare Birthplace Trust.

delights other people are visions of human aspiration, achievement and love (or perhaps unbridled power, rape and lust): Alexander and his paramour; Helen of Troy; and grapes grown by humans in accordance with nature – albeit on the other side of the world. Thus it is that the opening Chorus's protestations that the author has left aside the themes of war, love and 'audacious deeds', that he had covered in *Tamburlaine* (Chorus 1.1–5), are demonstrated as being disingenuous. Rather, this play is a continuation of these central themes in another key. Faustus's intellectual aspirations, however, are reduced to tricks on the body – the legerdemain of the conjurer – discomforting those who fail to take him seriously or who try to get one over on him.

But just as the Horse-courser comically fails to outwit Faustus in his bargain with him, so Faustus will be kept to his horrific bargain with the devil. Faustus's final speech is an agony of conflicted theology: he accepts the inevitability of damnation, and, briefly, the possibility of salvation; he wishes for Pythagorean '*metempsychosis*' (belief in the transmigration of souls), which he then confuses with the idea that animals have no souls and therefore no painful afterlife (compare 5.133.n). He curses his parents, then himself, then Lucifer (13.86–103). This speech is easier to read as a genuine philosophical problem in the A-text because it has not been preceded by yet another conventional argument between the Good and Evil angels, as it is in the B-text (Appendix 13). Faustus never gives up his very human struggle, demanding both 'God, look not so fierce on me' and 'Ugly hell, gape not', while trying a last ditch bargain, 'I'll burn my books' (13.108–11). Whether his final 'ah, Mephastophilis' is despair or ecstatic recognition is a production choice that does not have to be determined by the Chorus's conventional summing up.

The Vision of Helen

The most quoted lines in the play are those that relate to the appearance of Helen, the wife of the Spartan King Menelaus, whose abduction by the Trojan Paris sparked the ten-year siege of Troy: 'Was this the face that launched a thousand ships?' (12.89). The longing is palpable, but longing for what? A real woman? Or a woman from myth and literature? Here, she is presented by a spirit/devil, or rather, underneath the costume, an actor, and in Marlowe's day, a young male actor. The words that describe her are quotations from Marlowe's other plays, which in turn quote classical sources (see 12.89–108n).

Marlowe was no doubt playing games with all these various identities. But the dramaturgical complexity does not end there. The appearance of Helen is not Faustus's idea, but that of the two unnamed 'scholars', who are content to depart once they have merely seen this 'only paragon of excellence' (12.30). This is blasphemous, since in Christian terms if there is to be only one paragon it must be Christ, and it prompts the entrance of the Old Man whose repeated offer of salvation merely causes Faustus's renewed despair. Some editors follow the B-text in placing the stage direction in which Mephastophilis presents Faustus with a dagger so as to make it appear that it is *he* who tempts Faustus to despair, like a medieval Vice figure. The later position of this direction in the A-text of the play (which is followed in this edition), is more interesting. There, it comes in the margin *after* Faustus says his 'hour is come' (12.49), thus ironically confirming that Faustus is already in despair, and unexpectedly giving him the opportunity actually to kill himself. The effect is blackly humorous.

Having reconfirmed his pledge to Lucifer and spitefully asked Mephastophilis to torment the Old Man (which again Mephastophilis is powerless to do, 12.74–9), Faustus asks that Helen should be his paramour. She re-enters, and he kisses her: 'make me immortal with a kiss' (12.91). The attempt to save his soul in this manner prompts the re-entry in the A-text of the Old Man, who stands by, silently watching as Faustus's talk becomes literary fantasy. Faustus imagines himself as Paris wreaking destruction on town and heroes alike for an illicit love, and describes Helen as brighter and more lovely than Jupiter when he destroyed the mortal nymphs, his lovers. This ecstatic mixture of belief, desire, reality, myth, and gender identity defies explanation – as of course does faith itself, which is why it is called faith. But the Old Man's silent entrance twice in succession at the very moments when Helen's appearance satiates her onlookers (12.30; 12.95) functions as a visual comment, an unspoken question. It also puts him in the role of voyeur. The scene in the A-text concludes with the Old Man confronting the devils. He claims victory over them, 'Hence, hell, for hence I fly unto my God' (12.117), but since he and the devils exit by different doors, the *visual* message as to who is flying from whom is ambiguous.

This emotionally charged indeterminacy is why the play has so appealed to the doubts, fears and contradictions in late twentieth- and early twenty first-century western culture, and why it has prompted so many experimental productions. The staging of the central scenes in the play in which characters are now visible now invisible, now at the court of the emperor, now on the road home, with the horse courser and Faustus both on stage at once in slightly different locations, appeared inept to those commentators looking for rhetorical set-pieces and clear moral imperatives. But, in its understanding of the capability of theatre, and with its dangerous search for a mere fantasy, this play captures the conundrum of the unknowability of human existence. The ending may present conventional hell fire and the unequivocal morality of the final Chorus, yet that Chorus's very last couplet implies that Faustus will not be the last person to 'practise more than heavenly power permits' (13.118). The memories of slapstick and spectacle, as much as horror and tragedy, will allow audiences – should they so wish – to entertain a robust scepticism.

Early Performances

The preserved papers of Philip Henslowe, theatrical impresario and owner of the Rose Theatre, provide the dates for the earliest known performances of the play. They show that it was acted by the Lord Admiral's men on 30 September 1594, exactly sixteen months after Marlowe's death, and that it was a popular play. Henslowe records thirteen performances between that date and the end of 1595, usually with sizeable takings. In further performances the following year, the takings diminished, but the play remained popular.[11]

From a number of contemporary references to the play, we can tell that it was the special effects that sold this show. An inventory of the Admiral's Men's props in Henslowe's papers lists the dragon they had used 'in Fostes'.[12] Two authors of satirical attacks on abuses in London, who were themselves playwrights, rely on their readers' knowledge of the play in performance. Thomas Dekker, describing a pitched battle between the forces Poverty and Money in *The Seven Deadly Sinnes of London* (1606) writes, 'wild fire flew from one to another, like squibs when Doctor Faustus goes to the divell' (F4r). Thomas Middleton, in *The Blacke Booke* (1604), describes one of his characters leaping tousled out of bed with 'a head of hayre like one of the divells in *Doctor Faustus*, when the olde Theatre crackt and frighted the audience' (B4r). Theatre buildings at that time were often rickety and occasionally collapsed entirely, which the godly would put down to divine retribution,[13] but Faustus was notorious for a 'real' devil appearing onstage (see below, p. xxiii). Samuel Rowlands relates that Henslowe's son-in-law, Edward Alleyn, the lead actor of the Admiral's Men, and the first actor to play Faustus, performed the part in a surplice with a large cross on his breast.[14] It is impossible to tell whether

11 *Henslowe's Diary*, ed. Foakes and Rickert, 1961, pp. 24–36, 47, 54–5, 60.
12 *Henslowe's Diary*, ed. Foakes and Rickert, 1961, p. 320.
13 Puritan minister John Field in *A Godly Exhortation*, 1583, described the collapse of the Paris Garden bull ring in which many people were injured as a 'judgement of god' against those attending sports on a Sunday.
14 Samuel Rowlands, *The Knave of Clubbes*, 1609, D3.

this was worn as a superstitious actor's self-protection or as a canny actor manager's bid to add frisson and box-office value by encouraging such rumours.

Recent Stage History

Marlowe's *Faustus* has consistently attracted wildly differing interpretations, polarised between those who take an orthodox religious line on Faustus's rejection of salvation and those who stress the tragedy of his failed humanist intellectual aspirations. Productions have also tended to trim, alter, ignore or rewrite the comic scenes and, to an unusual extent, to reflect the cultural, moral and political outlooks of their own time. Clifford Williams's 1968 production for the RSC, for instance, was heralded by a frenzy of press speculation as to whether Helen really was going to appear fully naked; she did, in shiny, untouchable body make-up, to much admiration.

Charles Marowitz's production for the Glasgow Citizens, also in 1968, which toured several experimental theatre festivals in Europe, framed the play with a dialogue between Faustus and Robert Oppenheimer, inventor of the atomic bomb, on the responsibility of scientists for their inventions. The action took place in a courtroom, with Faustus on trial, and Marlowe's scenes staged as flashbacks.[15]

Of course, it is not scientists who are responsible for the (continuing) nuclear threat, but the governments and power groups that seek to deploy that science. Knowledge is neither moral nor immoral. It is what is done with knowledge that matters. Marlowe who it seems had lived his life on the furthest margins of power, understood this better than his commentators. The technology that enabled the industrial revolution of the eighteenth and nineteenth centuries was mostly in place when Marlowe was writing, but the application of that technology was in its infancy, confined to producing toys and entertainments for the courts of Europe. Faustus's tragedy is not so much that he is the flawed hero of post enlightenment science but that, given the nature of renaissance science, his achievements are put to such trivial uses.

By 2002, however, David Lan, director of a production at the Young Vic in London in which Jude Law played Faustus, was struck not so much by what Ben Jonson famously called 'Marlowe's mighty line'[16] but by the 'very unusual conversational tone of the play . . . very like the way people

---

15 Charles Marowitz, *'Hamlet'; and 'The Tragical History of Dr Faustus': a collage version of Shakespeare's play and a free adaptation of Marlowe's play*, 1970.
16 'To the memory of my beloved, the author Mr William Shakespeare', *Shakespeares Comedies, Histories, and Tragedies*, 1623, A4.

think about major scientific problems, such as what is the cosmos? What's the relationship between the little planet that we live on and the rest of the universe? Is there anything out there other than space and bits of metal junk? . . . it is a really good play to do now'.[17]

In the same year, a production for the Royal and Derngate Theatres in Northampton replaced the comic scenes with a new play-within-a-play written by Rupert Goold (who also directed) and Ben Power. This concerned BritArt stars Jake and Dinos Chapman, who had recently 'rectified' a set of 83 Goya etchings, *The Disasters of War,* by painting clowns' and puppies' heads over the heads of figures in the etchings, thereby creating a new work, *Insult to Injury.* Goya had made the series in response to Napoleon's invasion of Spain, the so-called Peninsular War, but it depicts the brutalities carried out on both sides and was deemed too sensitive to be published until 1863 – thirty five years after the artist's death. This particular set, printed from the original plates, was produced in 1937 as a protest against Fascist atrocities in the Spanish Civil War. In Goold and Power's play, the Chapmans invite Helena, a young photographer from Afghanistan, to record their actions, but she is horrified by what she sees as the desecration of the etchings and refuses; it is too close to her own experience, for she and her young brother had witnessed the destruction of the Bamiyan Buddhas by the Taliban in March 2001, and the boy had been killed.

Critics noted the exact parallel between what the Chapmans were doing to Goya and what the production was doing to Marlowe's play: for although the Goya set was printed from the original plates, in pristine condition, and very expensive, it was not unique, and its defacement into new, arguably more 'authentic' works (in the sense that the Chapmans had themselves painted the additions) equated with both the printing and the production history of Marlowe's play. For Goold and Power the question was 'is anything truly irrevocable or irreversible and how do we live with the consequences of our actions? For Faustus this is bound up with his eternal soul, for Jake and Dinos it's about the value of art and whether any work of art is sacred or permanent'.[18] As Jake and Dinos say in their play: 'JAKE: What is Hell? DINOS: Hell? Hell is having nothing to

17 Young Vic, Doctor Faustus resource pack, www.youngvic.org/assets/attachments/ resource-packs/doctor-faustus.pdf, p. 30, accessed 11.7.2007.

18 For images of Goold's production see http://www.headlongtheatre.co.uk/prod_faustus_ gallery.html, accessed 6.1.2008. The production, originating at the Derngate Theatre Northampton, was revived at Hampstead Theatre, 2006, and subsequently in a touring production, Autumn 2007 (dir. Steve Marmion); see Rupert Goold and Ben Power after Christopher Marlowe, *Faustus,* 2007; Jake and Dinos Chapman's etchings, *Insult to Injury,* were published by Paragon Press.

say.' The production ends with a projection informing the audience that in 2004 another Chapman brothers work entitled 'Hell' was consumed in a warehouse fire, along with many other examples of contemporary British art.

A Note on the Text

Marlowe's *Dr Faustus* has come down to us in two very different versions, printed in 1604 (the so-called 'A-text') and 1616 (the 'B-text'). The A-text is some 676 lines shorter than the B-text and was at one time thought to represent a maimed and truncated version of the play. The B-text contains extensions to the satirical anti-catholic material in the play – including an episode at the papal court, where the philosopher Bruno is accused of heresy. The B-text also contains additions to the horse-courser story; a greatly extended version of the incident in which Faustus places horns on the head of a knight at the court of the Holy Roman Emperor; and rather more in the way of devilish spectacle. Extensive smaller changes throughout result in a text that is more orthodox – in terms of the doctrine of the early seventeenth-century English church – than that in the A-text. Significantly, it is the A-text alone which dares to state that divinity is 'basest' of the various arts, 'Unpleasant, harsh, contemptible, and vile' (1.108–9). The general consensus now amongst scholars is that while the A-text may contain some minor alterations and topical allusions (e.g. the reference to Dr Lopus, 10.123), which can only have been added after Marlowe's death, it must be the earliest extant version of the play, while the extensive differences in the B-text probably represent the revisions and 'adicyons' made by William Byrde and Samuel Rowley, for which they were paid £4 by the theatre impresario Philip Henslowe in 1604.[19] The A-text therefore forms the basis for this edition.

There are, however, problems with the structure of the material in the A-text that an editor needs to consider. Two scenes concerning Robin Ostler run consecutively in the A-text, immediately after Chorus 3. This must be wrong since there needs to be a time-lapse between them, and the function of Chorus 3 is to introduce a scene at the Emperor's court. Likewise, the scene in which Faustus sells his soul to the devil runs continuously into the scene with the Seven Deadly Sins. This is unsatisfactory since the line 'Long ere this' and the ravishing recollection that Faustus has been sung to by Homer and heard the music that built the walls of Thebes (7.24–30 in this edition) implies that, by the time of the Seven Deadly Sins episode, his pact with the devil is already of some

19 *Henslowe's Diary*, ed. Foakes and Rickert, 1961, p. 206.

duration. The B-text gives a clue to a solution since there the scene is split by the insertion of a short version of Chorus 2 in which Wagner prematurely describes the journey to Rome. The long version of that speech, however, also occurs in the appropriate place in the B-text. The duplication of this Chorus in the B-text is an error, but the splitting of the scene into two is probably correct.

In the previous New Mermaid edition of *Dr Faustus*, Roma Gill keeps the long Faustus Mephastophilis scene undivided, inserts the first Robin scene immediately after it, and places the second Robin scene (with the goblet) after the papal banquet. This revised New Mermaids edition follows Bevington and Rasmussen in placing the first Robin scene so as to split the long Faustus Mephastophilis scene into two.[20] Treated in this way, both Robin scenes form satirical commentaries on the Faustus scenes that have preceded them. Bevington and Rasmussen's explanation for the placing of these scenes in the A-text is that they must have been written out on loose sheets of paper – perhaps because they were written by a collaborator, and not by Marlowe – and were as a consequence misplaced in the manuscript.

Date and Sources

The many stories about Faustus, many of them similar to stories about other infamous magicians, were brought together and published in Frankfurt by Johann Spies in 1587.[21] One of the first international bestsellers, this, the so-called Faustbuch was soon published in translation in Dutch and French. The first surviving English version appeared in 1592 as *The Historie of the Damnable Life and Deserved Death of Doctor John Faustus*, but it is likely that this is a second edition since it claims on its titlepage to have been 'amended according to the true copie printed at Frankfurt'. It was translated by one P.F., about whom nothing else is known, except the claim, also on the title page, that he was a gentleman.

Verbal echoes of lines found only in the A-text can be found in *The Taming of A Shrew*, an anonymous play that may be a source for, or a debased version of, Shakespeare's *The Taming of the Shrew*. This was published in 1594, the year of the first recorded performances of *Faustus* (see above p. xix). Nevertheless, *Faustus* may well have been in existence by about 1589, for William Prynne much later repeated hearsay that an extra devil had appeared on stage during a performance at the

---

20 *Doctor Faustus: A- and B- texts (1604, 1616)*, ed. David Bevington and Eric Rasmussen, 1993, pp. 64–77.

21 *Historia von D. Johan Fausten*, Frankfurt: Johann Spies, 1587.

22 William Prynne, *Histriomastix*, 1633, p. 556. A similar event is said to have occurred in Exeter.

Belsavage,[22] a playhouse that is not thought to have been in use after 1589. This early date is not impossible if it is assumed that Marlowe had had access to a version of *The Damnable Life* published earlier than the extant 1592 edition, or that he knew one of the European editions. The first printed reference to Faustus in English in fact occurs in Ludwig Lavater's *Of Ghostes and Spirites walking by nyght* (1572): 'What straunge things are reported of one Faustus a German, which he did in these our dayes by inchauntments' and dismisses 'Magitians, jugglers, inchanters, and necromanciers' as 'no other than servants of the Divel' (p. 170).

The *Ballad of the Life and Death of Doctor Faustus the great Cunngerer* registered by the printer Richard Jones on 28 February 1589 attests to the popularity of the Faustus story in England just two years after the publication of the German Faustbuch, and the most likely reason for such popularity at this date is the existence of Marlowe's very popular play. No copy of this ballad survives, unless a ballad much reprinted in the seventeenth century is identical with it. This was advertised to be sung to 'Fortune my foe', a ubiquitous tune, often used for processions to the gallows. Other later ballads were published with instructions they should be sung to the tune of 'Faustus' – testament to the extraordinary popularity of the Faustus story in ballad as in play.

The Author

The facts about Christopher Marlowe's life, as with the life of any other Englishman of his period and class, are few. The parish records of St George's in Canterbury show that he was baptised in February 1564 (a few months before William Shakespeare), that he was the son of Katherine and John Marlowe (a shoemaker), and that he had three sisters. The family was relatively poor and two of his sisters were known to the authorities: Dorothy for matrimonial offences; and Ann as a 'scold, common swearer and blasphemer of the name of god'.[23] But in 1578 Christopher won a scholarship to the King's School in Canterbury, and two years later, a Bishop Matthew Parker scholarship to Corpus Christi College, Cambridge. The Parker scholarships were given to 'the best and aptest schollers' from poorer families and, ideally, to those who could also sing well and write poetry.[24] Awarded for three years in the first instance, the scholarship could be extended to six for those intending to take holy orders. Marlowe held his for the full six years.

This education will have given Marlowe a thorough grounding in Latin grammar, rhetoric and logic. His schooling will have been largely devoted

23 William Urry, 'Marlowe and Canterbury', *TLS* 13 February 1964.
24 Annie Wraight and Virginia Stern, *In search of Christopher Marlowe*, 1965, p. 63.

to the process of double translation – from Latin into English, and then back into Latin.[25] He will have read widely, both in classical literature and in works of divinity, and will have progressed through participation in disputations, which involved arguing a given case in divinity or philosophy according to strict rules of exposition and evidence. Both school and university may also have offered scholarly recreations, such as acting in plays (in Latin as well as English), or writing new versions of well-known stories, as advocated by the great humanist writer and educator, Erasmus.[26] Marlowe's poetry – the wonderfully passionate Ovidian poem *Hero and Leander*, and his translations of Lucan – attest to this education, and demonstrate that he had the inventiveness and imagination to make it his own.

At Cambridge, the account books for the buttery at Corpus Christi College show that in his first year his purchases of food and drink were both moderate and regular. But in 1584–5 there are no entries for 32 weeks, which suggests an absence from the university. Subsequently, he spent more freely on drink than his scholarship should have allowed. Internal references in some of the plays including some Parisian hearsay in *The Massacre at Paris*, and perhaps the reference in *Faustus* to the Spanish fireship used in the siege of Antwerp, may suggest that he was in France and the Netherlands at that time.[27] Perhaps as a result of such absence, the university tried to prevent him from sitting his MA degree. Records show that the Privy Council sent a letter to the college interceding on his behalf, and stating that he 'had done her Majestie good service and deserved to be rewarded for his faithfull dealinge'. Their Lordships had heard the rumour that he had intended to go 'beyond the seas to Rheims', where there was a college which trained English students for the Catholic priesthood and thus for a life of treasonous recusancy back in England. They 'thought good to certefie that he had no such intent, but that in all his accons [actions] he had behaved him selfe orderlie and discreetlie', and requested that he be granted his degree 'because it was not Her Majesties pleasure that anie one emploied as he had been in matters touching the benefitt of his Countrie should be defamed by those that are ignorant in th'affaires he went about.'[28] His MA was duly awarded.

The Privy Council interest in this lowly student suggests that he had been employed by the government. Sir Francis Walsingham, Elizabeth's

25 See T.W.Baldwin, *William Shakespere's Small Latin and Lesse Greeke*, 2 vols., 1966.
26 Erasmus, 'Method of Study' in *Collected Works of Erasmus*, ed. Craig R. Thompson, vol. 24, 1978, p. 681.
27 Park Honan, *Christopher Marlowe: Poet and Spy*, 2005, pp. 147–8.
28 *Acts of the Privy Council*, VI, 29 June 1587.

chief minister, and the man she called her 'eyes', ran probably the most sophisticated secret service in Europe, and Francis's kinsman, Thomas, was Marlowe's patron. But it is important not to overstate this point. Any young English gentleman who travelled abroad was likely to have been asked to bring home 'intelligence' of what was happening in the various countries of Europe.

Thereafter, Marlowe was regularly in trouble with the law. On one occasion he was bound over to keep the peace; on another he was arrested for killing a man in a street brawl – for which he was soon released, which adds to the suspicion that he was under government protection. Obviously no stranger to violence, Marlowe was fatally stabbed through the eye at a house in Deptford, the naval town on the south bank of the Thames near London, on Wednesday 30 May 1593. His murderer, Ingram Frizar, who also seems to have had connections with the security services, claimed self-defence and was acquitted. But by the time of his death, at the age of just 29, Marlowe had completed five of the most famous plays in the English language, the two parts of *Tamburlaine*; *The Jew of Malta*; *Edward II*; and *Doctor Faustus*, as well as the lesser known *Dido, Queen of Carthage*, and *The Massacre at Paris*, the latter concerning the St Bartholomew's day massacre of Protestants in France. At the point when he died, Marlowe was a more influential and more imitated poet and playwright than his contemporary, Shakespeare.

As far as *Faustus* is concerned, the most suggestive aspects of Marlowe's biography are his involvement with the shady Richard Baines, and the accusation, extracted under torture from the playwright Thomas Kyd, that Marlowe was an 'atheist'. Baines too had been at Cambridge and seems to have been rather ineptly spying for Walsingham at the English College at Rheims in 1578, where he became a priest, before being exposed, imprisoned and tortured by them in 1582.[29] He was also in Flushing with Marlowe and one Gifford Gilbert in 1591. Baines approached the governor of the town, Sir Robert Sidney, accusing Gilbert of counterfeiting money, and both Gilbert and Marlowe were arrested. But judging by his letter about them to the Privy Council, Sidney had no real conviction that they had committed a crime. Only one coin had been produced and that, being pewter, was identifiable as a fake 'with half an eye'. Both Baines and Marlowe had also accused each other of going to the enemy at Rome, but Marlowe was at liberty in England shortly afterwards. Baines later wrote a note to the Privy Council recounting what Marlowe had supposedly said in his hearing, which was transcribed

29 Park Honan, *Christopher Marlowe: Poet and Spy*, 2005, p. 144.

shortly after Marlowe's death. The note is evidently malicious yet it also sounds like a fairly accurate report of what a clever, intellectually confident, perhaps brash, and probably drunk young man might say: among other things, that the 'beginning of Religioun was only to keep men in awe'; that 'if he were put to write a new Religion, he would undertake both a more Excellent and Admirable methode and that all the new testament is filthily written'; that he 'had as good Right to Coine [i.e. mint money] as the Queen of England'; and that they who 'love not tobacco and Boyes were fools', which is perhaps a joke on the blasphemous comment that immediately precedes it in the note, that John the Baptist had used Christ sodomitically.[30]

Marlowe's irascible nature does not make him the ideal spy, but the suggestion that he might have been one, and his tragically early death, appealed to the generation of critics and writers who lived through the Cold War. He became the glamorous subject of a number of novels.[31] In 1953 during building works at Corpus Christi, Cambridge, a sixteenth-century picture of a young gentleman wearing a slashed red velvet doublet and lawn collar was discovered on a skip. Bearing both the date (1585) and the age (21) of the sitter, but no name, it was quickly claimed as a portrait of the poet. The fashionable and expensive cut of his clothes was taken as evidence of the government service, and the government service was used to explain the clothes – in an entirely circular argument. Much was made of the enigmatic smile and the hidden left hand, and the motto *Quod me nutrit me destruit* ('That which feeds me destroys me'). In style, clothing and date it is very similar to the 'Grafton portrait' previously claimed to be of Shakespeare. But these identifications attest to a romantic desire to make tangibly handsome heartthrobs of two culturally important figures, about whom less is known than we would like. The pictures are probably no more than conventional portraits of two wealthy but anonymous young men.

30 Christopher Marlowe, *Doctor Faustus*, ed. David Scott Kastan (2005), pp. 127–9.
31 e.g. Anthony Burgess, *A Dead Man in Deptford*, 1993; Charles Nichol, *The Reckoning: The Murder of Christopher Marlowe*, 1992.

FURTHER READING

Editions

Doctor Faustus, ed. David Scott Kastan, 2005

Doctor Faustus: A and B-texts (1604, 1616), ed. David Bevington and Eric Rasmussen, 1993

The Complete Works of Christopher Marlowe, ed. Roma Gill, 5 vols., 1986–98, 2: *Dr Faustus*, 1990

Dr Faustus, ed. Michael H. Keefer, 1991

Critical works and biography

Alexander, Nigel, 'The Performance of Christopher Marlowe's *Dr Faustus*', *Proceedings of the British Academy*, Vol. LVII, 1972

Dabbs, Thomas, *Reforming Marlowe, The Nineteenth-Century Canonization of a Renaissance Dramatist*, 1991

Downie, J.A. and J.T. Parnell, *Constructing Christopher Marlowe*, 2000

Grantley, Darryll, *Christopher Marlowe and English Renaissance Culture*, 1999

Healy, Thomas, '*Dr Faustus*' in Patrick Cheney, ed. *The Cambridge Companion to Marlowe*, 2004, pp. 174–92

Honan, Park, *Christopher Marlowe: Poet and Spy*, 2005

Hopkins, Lisa, *Christopher Marlowe: A Literary Life*, 2000

Jump, John D., ed., *Marlowe: Doctor Faustus: A Casebook*, 1969

Leech, Clifford, *Christopher Marlowe: Poet for the Stage*, 1986

Levin, H., *The Overreacher: A Study of Christopher Marlowe*, 1954

Lunney, Ruth, *Marlowe and the Popular Tradition*, 2002

Maclure, Millar, *Christopher Marlowe: The Collected Critical Heritage, 1588–1896*, 1995

Mangan, Michael, *Marlowe's Dr Faustus*, 1987

Nutall, A.D. *The Alternative Trinity: Gnostic Heresy in Marlowe, Milton and Blake*, 2007

Parker, John, *The Aesthetics of Antichrist: from Christian Drama to Christopher Marlowe*, 2007

Riggs, David, *The World of Christopher Marlowe*, 2004

Tydeman, William, *Dr Faustus: Text and Performance*, 1984

Weil, Judith, *Christopher Marlowe: Merlin's Prophet*, 1977

ABBREVIATIONS

I have followed the usual practice in referring to the seventeenth-century editions of *Dr Faustus*: 'A' indicates substantial agreement between all the A Texts, which are referred to separately on occasion as A1 (1604), A2 (1609), and A3 (1611); the B texts (1616, 1619, 1620, 1624, 1628, and 1631) are similarly distinguished. Modern editions are referred to as follows:

Boas	*The Tragical History of Doctor Faustus*, edited by F. S. Boas (1932)
Bullen	*The Works of Christopher Marlowe*, edited by A. H. Bullen (1885)
Dyce	*The Complete Works of Christopher Marlowe*, edited by A. Dyce (1850)
Greg	*Marlowe's Dr Faustus' 1604-1616: Parallel Texts*, edited by W. W. Greg (1950)
Jump	*Dr Faustus*, edited by John D. Jump (1962)

Other works frequently referred to are:

EFB	The *English Faust Book*, the name given to Marlowe's source [*The Historic of the damnable life, and deserved death of Doctor Iohn Faustus*, translated by P. F. (1592)]
Kocher	P. H. Kocher, *Christopher Marlowe* (1946)

Names of periodicals are abbreviated:

E.L.H.	*English Literary History*
E.S.	*English Studies*
E & S	*Essays and Studies*
M.L.N.	*Modern Language Notes*
M.L.Q.	*Modern Language Quarterly*
M.L.R.	*Modern Language Review*
N & Q	*Notes and Queries*
P.Q.	*Philological Quarterly*
R.E.S.	*Review of English Studies*
T.L.S.	*Times Literary Supplement*

Quotations from other plays by Marlowe are taken from *The Plays of Chrisopher Marlowe*, edited by Roma Gill (1971); those from Shakespeare's plays are from the Riverside edition.

The title page of the first printed text of *Dr Faustus*, the A-text (1604, reprinted 1609, 1611). The printer's device is described by R. B. McKerrow (*Printers' and Publishers' Devices in England and Scotland, 1485–1640*, 1913, p. 142) as 'A boy with wings upon his right arm and with his left hand holding, or fastened to, a weight', the emblem signifying talent frustrated by poverty. It was not unique to *Dr Faustus*: the printer, Valentine Simmes, had used it on several other books, including the 1597 quarto of Shakespeare's *Richard II*. Reprinted by kind permission of the Bodleian Library, Oxford.

THE
TRAGICALL
History of D. Fauſtus.

As it hath bene Acted by the Right
Honorable the Earle of Nottingham his ſeruants.

Written by Ch. Marl.

LONDON
Printed by V. S. for Thomas Buſhell. 1604.

DRAMATIS PERSONAE

CHORUS

DR JOHN FAUSTUS
WAGNER, *his servant, a student*
VALDES
CORNELIUS } *his friends, magicians*
THREE SCHOLARS

THE GOOD ANGEL
THE EVIL ANGEL
MEPHASTOPHILIS
LUCIFER
BELZEBUB
OLD MAN

THE CLOWN
ROBIN
RAFE } *ostlers at an inn*

VINTNER
HORSE-COURSER

THE POPE
THE CARDINAL OF LORRAINE

THE EMPEROR CHARLES V
A KNIGHT *at the emperor's court*
DUKE OF VANHOLT
DUCHESS OF VANHOLT

MEPHASTOPHILIS This version of the character's name is used consistently throughout the A-text; the B-text spelling, 'Mephostophilis', is used in the Appendix of scenes from that text. William Empson has a note on the various spellings in *Faustus and the Censor* (1987), pp. 45–6n

Spirits presenting
THE SEVEN DEADLY SINS
    PRIDE
    COVETOUSNESS
    WRATH
    ENVY
    GLUTTONY
    SLOTH
    LECHERY
ALEXANDER THE GREAT *and his* PARAMOUR
HELEN OF TROY

Attendants, Friars, and Devils

[Chorus 1]

Enter CHORUS

CHORUS

Not marching now in fields of Thrasimene,
Where Mars did mate the Carthaginians,
Nor sporting in the dalliance of love,
In courts of kings where state is overturned,
Nor in the pomp of proud audacious deeds,   5
Intends our Muse to daunt his heavenly verse:
Only this (Gentlemen) we must perform,
The form of Faustus' fortunes good or bad.
To patient judgements we appeal our plaud,
And speak for Faustus in his infancy: 10
Now is he born, his parents base of stock,
In Germany, within a town called Rhodes;

---

s.d. CHORUS Following the example of classical drama, many Elizabethan plays began
       with a Chorus or Prologue to introduce the action, and sometimes comment on the
       author's skill and the nature of his writing. The Chorus takes the persona of an actor
       in the company presenting the play, possibly the actor playing Faustus's servant Wagner,
       see l. 28n and Chorus 2.0n (p. 48).

1–5   The Chorus speaks of plays already performed, but – whether these were written by
       Marlowe or merely part of the company's repertoire – the references are unclear.
       There is no trace of any play showing the victory of the Carthaginians under Hannibal
       at Lake Thrasymenus in 217 B.C.; and any number of plays (including Marlowe's
       own *Edward II*) could be said to show 'the dalliance of love' in royal courts.

  2   *Mars* the Roman god of war
       mate ally himself with

  3   *dalliance* frivolity

  6   *our Muse* our poet; the Chorus is speaking on behalf of the acting company
       daunt A (vaunt B) a) control, tame, subdue, b) dally, caress. This wordplay immediately
       introduces a note of irony. The Chorus denies that the play is about war or love but
       this pun suggests it will combine both heroics and sensuality, and outdo any previous
       play. The B-text's 'vaunt' simply means 'show off'

  9   *appeal our plaud* ask for applause

 12   *Rhodes* Roda, since 1922 Stadtroda (in Germany)

Of riper years to Wittenberg he went,
Whereas his kinsmen chiefly brought him up.
So soon he profits in divinity, 15
The fruitful plot of scholarism graced,
That shortly he was graced with doctor's name,
Excelling all, whose sweet delight disputes
In heavenly matters of theology,
Till swollen with cunning of a self-conceit, 20
His waxen wings did mount above his reach,
And melting heavens conspired his overthrow.
For falling to a devilish exercise,
And glutted more with learning's golden gifts,
He surfeits upon cursed necromancy: 25
Nothing so sweet as magic is to him,
Which he prefers before his chiefest bliss.
And this the man that in his study sits. *Exit*

13 *Wittenberg* B Hamlet's university, and Luther's, was the home of scepticism; but this
   Wittenberg is, in all outward appearances, Marlowe's own Cambridge. The A-text
   has 'Wertenberg[e]' here (and throughout. 1.89; 1.114; 10.92; 12.97; 13.17), i e. the
   Duchy of Wurtemburg, a territory rather than a university town. The two names were
   often confused, as once in Marlowe's English source, but see Introduction p. ix.
14 *Whereas* where
16 'a credit to the rich discipline of academic studies'
17 *graced* At Cambridge, an official 'grace' permits a candidate to proceed to his degree;
   Marlowe's name is entered in the Grace Book for 1584 and 1587.
18 *whose sweet delight disputes* whose great pleasure is in academic debate
20 *cunning* a) skill, knowledge, b) specifically magical skill. The word had also begun
   to acquire its modern sense of craftiness or deceitfulness
   self-conceit a) pride in his own abilities, b) individual thinking, unregulated by religion
   or convention, c) thinking himself to be something other than he is (i.e. Icarus, ll.
   21–2), d) 'self-fashioned'
21 *waxen wings* In Greek mythology, Icarus flew too near the sun on wings of wax; they
   melted, and he fell into the sea. The fall of Icarus became a popular Renaissance
   emblem throughout Europe.
24 *more* A (now B)
27 *chiefest bliss* i.e. hope of life after death
28 *this the man* This seems to be the cue for the Chorus to draw aside a curtain and
   disclose Faustus in his study, thus perhaps falling into his role as Faustus's servant.

[Scene 1]

Enter FAUSTUS *in his study*

FAUSTUS

Settle thy studies, Faustus, and begin
To sound the depth of that thou wilt profess:
Having commenced, be a divine in show,
Yet level at the end of every art,
And live and die in Aristotle's works.   5
Sweet *Analytics*, 'tis thou hast ravished me:
Bene disserere est finis logices.
Is to dispute well logic's chiefest end?
Affords this art no greater miracle?
Then read no more, thou hast attained the end;   10
A greater subject fitteth Faustus' wit.
Bid *on kai me on* farewell; Galen come:

2   *sound* measure
    profess specialize in, study and teach
3   *commenced* graduated; a Cambridge term
    divine theologian
    in show in appearance
4   consider the purpose of every discipline
5–37 In his survey of human scholarship Faustus resembles the protagonist of Lyly's
    Euphues (1578) who determines to return to the university:
        Philosophic, Phisicke, Divinitie, shal be my studie. O ye hidden secrets of Nature,
        the expresse image of morall venues, the equall ballaunce of Justice, the medicines
        to heale all diseases, how they beginne to delyght me. The *Axiomaes* of *Aristotle,*
        the *Maxims* of *Justinian,* the *Aphorismes* of *Galen,* have sodaynelye made such a
        breache into my minde, that I seem onely to desire them which did onely earst
        detest them.   *Euphues,* ed. Bond (1902), i.241
  5–7 Aristotle had been the dominant figure in the university curriculum since the thirteenth
    century, but in Marlowe's day his supremacy was challenged by the intellectual reformer
    Petrus Ramus. *Analytics* is the name given to two of Aristotle's works on the nature of
    proof in argument, but the definition of logic in line 7 comes in fact from Ramus'
    Dialecticae. Ramus, his ideas, and his violent death are displayed in Marlowe's *Massacre*
    at Paris
10 *the* A (that B)
12 *on kai me on* being and not being. A1 prints a jumble of letters, 'Oncaymaeon', which
    later editions, trying to make some sense out of them, changed to 'Oeconomy'. Bullen
    recognized the A-text's apparent gibberish as a transliteration of the Greek phrase,
    from a work attributed to the philosopher Georgias of Leontini (*c.* 483–376 B.C.)
    Galen a second-century Greek physician who was accepted as an authority on medical
    science throughout the Middle Ages

Seeing, *ubi desinit philosophus, ibi incipit medicus.*
Be a physician, Faustus, heap up gold,
And be eternized for some wondrous cure.   15
Summum bonum medicinae sanitas:
The end of physic is our body's health.
Why Faustus, hast thou not attained that end?
Is not thy common talk sound aphorisms?
Are not thy bills hung up as monuments,   20
Whereby whole cities have escaped the plague,
And thousand desperate maladies been eased?
Yet art thou still but Faustus, and a man.
Wouldst thou make man to live eternally,
Or, being dead, raise them to life again,   25
Then this profession were to be esteemed.
Physic farewell! Where is Justinian?
Si una eademque res legatur duobus,
Alter rem alter valorem rei, etc.

13   *ubi ... medicus* 'since the doctor starts where the philosopher leaves off'; Aristotle,
      De Sensu et Sensibili, ch 1, 436a
14   *heap up gold* The association of gold and the medical profession is an old one;
      Shakespeare mentions the use of gold for 'Preserving life in med'cine potable' (*2*
      Henry IV, IV. v. 162). Faustus, however, is thinking of the profit to be gained – like
      Chaucer's Physician in *The Canterbury Tales*:
          For gold in phisik is a cordial,
          Therefore he lovede gold in special.   (Prologue, 444–5)
15   *eternized* immortalized
16   Aristotle, *Nicomachean Ethics*, 1094. a. 8; Faustus translates in line 17
19   Faustus ranks himself with Hippocrates, whose *Aphorismes* was the most famous of
      medical textbooks.
      sound aphorisms well-founded maxims or concise expressions of scientific principles
      particularly of a medical nature (after the well-known *Aphorisms* of Hippocrates, a Greek
      physician of the 4th century B.C.). The B-text has 'found' i.e. considered to be 'aphorisms'.
20   *bills* writings, perhaps specifically prescriptions or advertisements
      monuments a) memorials, commemorations, b) portents, warnings, c) legal documents
21   *Whereby ... plague* It seems that his writings are considered to have prophylactic
      powers.
24–5 *Wouldst ... man* A (Could'st ... men B). Since Faustus is still only a man and not a
      god (see ll. 62–3), there would be no relative advantage for him in making mankind
      live for ever. By contrast, the B-text smoothes out the blasphemy of this line (since
      in Christian theology only Christ can raise the dead) by accepting that the goal is
      impossible.
27   Justinian was a Roman emperor of the sixth century A.D., who re-organized the
      whole of Roman Law.
28–9 'If one and the same thing is bequeathed to two persons, one should have the thing
      itself, the other the value of the thing': Justinian, *Institutes*, ii. 20.

A pretty case of paltry legacies: 30
Exhereditare filium non potest pater nisi . . .
Such is the subject of the Institute,
And universal body of the Church:
His study fits a mercenary drudge
Who aims at nothing but external trash!   35
Too servile and illiberal for me.
When all is done, divinity is best:
Jerome's Bible, Faustus, view it well:
Stipendium peccati mors est: ha! *Stipendium, etc.*
The reward of sin is death? That's hard.   40
Si peccasse negamus, fallimur, et nulla est in nobis veritas
If we say that we have no sin,
We deceive ourselves, and there's no truth in us.
Why then belike we must sin,
And so consequently die.   45
Ay, we must die an everlasting death.
What doctrine call you this? *Che serà, serà*:
What will be, shall be! Divinity, adieu!
These metaphysics of magicians,
And necromantic books are heavenly!   50

31   'A father cannot disinherit his son unless . . .': Justinian, ii. 13
32–3 *subject . . . Church* Faustus sneers that Justinian's book concerns merely inheritance
     and property law (i.e. 'external trash', l. 35). Punning on the overall title of Justinian's
     work (*Corpus Juris*, i.e. 'Body of the Law'), he suggests that this is a preoccupation
     of Christians generally (the 'body of the Church'), since Christian canon law was
     based on Justinian.
32   *Institute* element of instruction, or basic principles of a body of knowledge, hence
     the title of the legal textbook, *Institutes*, which was one part of Justinian's project to
     codify Roman Law
33   *Church* A (law B)
34   *His study* A (This study B)
     mercenary drudge wage slave
36   *Too servile* B (The devil A)
     illiberal Faustus compares the mercenary concerns of the lawyers with the culturally
     enriching studies of the 'liberal arts'.
38   *Jerome's Bible* the Vulgate, prepared mainly by St Jerome; but the texts that Faustus
     quotes are not in the Latin of the Vulgate
39   Romans vi, 23; Faustus reads only half the verse: the quotation should continue 'but
     the gift of God is eternal life through Jesus Christ our Lord'.
41–3 *Si peccasse . . . us* 1 John 1, 8 'If we say that we have no sin, we deceive ourselves, and
     the truth is not in us.' Verse 9 continues 'If we confess our sins, he is faithful and just
     to forgive us our sins, and to cleanse us from all unrighteousness.' By again making
     only a partial reading, Faustus fails to register the offered comfort.

Lines, circles, schemes, letters and characters!
Ay, these are those that Faustus most desires.
O what a world of profit and delight,
Of power, of honour, of omnipotence
Is promised to the studious artisan!   55
All things that move between the quiet poles
Shall be at my command: emperors and kings
Are but obeyed in their several provinces,
Nor can they raise the wind, or rend the clouds;
But his dominion that exceeds in this   60
Stretcheth as far as doth the mind of man:
A sound magician is a mighty god.
Here Faustus, try thy brains to gain a deity.
Wagner,

Enter WAGNER

commend me to my dearest friends,
The German Valdes, and Cornelius,   65
Request them earnestly to visit me.
WAGNER
I will sir.   *Exit*
FAUSTUS
Their conference will be a greater help to me,
Than all my labours, plod I ne'er so fast.

Enter the GOOD ANGEL *and the* EVIL ANGEL

51 *schemes* ed. (scenes A; *om,* B); rhetorical figures, astronomical diagrams (see John
    Harvey, *An Astrological Addition,* 1583, B5)
    characters symbols, astrological signs
55 *artisan* craftsman
56 *quiet poles* the poles of the universe, quiet because unmoving
58 *several* respective
59–62 Compare the description of God in Jeremiah x, 13: 'He giveth by his voice the
    multitude of waters in the heaven, and he causeth the clouds to ascend from the
    ends of the earth: he turneth lightnings to rain, and bringeth forth the wind out of
    his treasures.'
60 *exceeds* excels
    this i.e. this magic art
63 *try* A (tire B)
64 s.d. Although both A- and B-texts agree in placing this s.d. after line 63, sixteenth-
    century printers would find it more economical not to split the line. Wagner enters
    because he is called, not on his own accord.

9

GOOD ANGEL

   O Faustus, lay that damned book aside,   70
   And gaze not on it, lest it tempt thy soul,
   And heap God's heavy wrath upon thy head:
   Read, read the Scriptures; that is blasphemy.

EVIL ANGEL

   Go forward, Faustus, in that famous art,
   Wherein all nature's treasury is contained: 75
   Be thou on earth as Jove is in the sky,
   Lord and commander of these elements.

                                            Exeunt

FAUSTUS

   How am I glutted with conceit of this!
   Shall I make spirits fetch me what I please,
   Resolve me of all ambiguities,   80
   Perform what desperate enterprise I will?
   I'll have them fly to India for gold,
   Ransack the ocean for orient pearl,
   And search all corners of the new found world
   For pleasant fruits and princely delicates.   85
   I'll have them read me strange philosophy,
   And tell the secrets of all foreign kings;
   I'll have them wall all Germany with brass,
   And make swift Rhine circle fair Wittenberg;

76 *Jove* The names of the pagan deities were frequently attributed to the Christian God; there is special force in this coming from the Evil Angel.
77 *these elements* the four elements – earth, air, fire, and water – of which the world was made
78 *glutted with conceit* drunk with the thought
80 *Resolve . . . ambiguities* reduce my doubts to certainties; solve my problems
81 *desperate* a) dangerous, b) reckless, with the sense of despairing, which is a denial of Christian salvation
83 *orient pearl* The most precious pearls were from the Indian Ocean.
84 *new found* newly discovered
85 *delicates* delicacies
86 *read me* teach me
88 *wall . . . brass* Friar Bacon, in Greene's *Friar Bacon and Friar Bungay* (before 1592) intended to 'circle England round with brass' (ii. 29) when his magic schemes reached fruition.
89 *Wittenberg* B (Wertenberge A). Wittenberg in fact stands on the Elbe; it is the Duchy of Württemberg that is bordered by the southern Rhine (see Chorus 1.13n).

I'll have them fill the public schools with silk,   90
Wherewith the students shall be bravely clad.
I'll levy soldiers with the coin they bring,
And chase the Prince of Parma from our land,
And reign sole king of all our provinces.
Yea, stranger engines for the brunt of war   95
Than was the fiery keel at Antwerp's bridge,
I'll make my servile spirits to invent.
Come German Valdes and Cornelius,
And make me blest with your sage conference.

Enter VALDES *and* CORNELIUS

Valdes, sweet Valdes, and Cornelius,   100
Know that your words have won me at the last
To practise magic and concealed arts;
Yet not your words only, but mine own fantasy,
That will receive no object for my head,
But ruminates on necromantic skill.   105
Philosophy is odious and obscure,
Both law and physic are for petty wits;

90   *public schools* university lecture rooms
      silk Dyce (skill Qq (all quartos)); in Marlowe's day, undergraduates were ordered to dress
      in woollen cloth, not silk.
91   *bravely* smartly
92   *coin they bring* Spirits were deemed to know the whereabouts of hidden treasure.
93–6 The Prince of Parma was Spanish governor-general of the United Provinces of the
      Netherlands, 1579–92, and feared in Protestant England. The bridge he built across
      the Scheldt during his siege of Antwerp was destroyed by *fiery keel* (fireship) on
      4 April 1585.
94   *our* A (the B)
95   *engines* machines
      brunt assault
102 *concealed* occult
103 *fantasy* a) in scholastic philosophy, the faculty whereby objects are conceived,
      b) imagination
103–5 i.e. Faustus is becoming wrapped up in his own inner thoughts and is finding it
      difficult to think about the external, material, or objective world.
104 *object* a) in metaphysics, a material thing external to the mind or to the subjective
      self, b) with a pun on 'objection'
105 *ruminates* meditates deeply, often used at this period with a sense of dark or
      dangerous melancholy
      necromantic skill magic that works through conjuring and controlling spirits

Divinity is basest of the three,
Unpleasant, harsh, contemptible and vile.
'Tis magic, magic that hath ravished me   110
Then, gentle friends, aid me in this attempt,
And I, that have with concise syllogisms
Gravelled the pastors of the German church,
And made the flowering pride of Wittenberg
Swarm to my problems, as the infernal spirits   115
On sweet Musaeus when he came to hell,
Will be as cunning as Agrippa was,
Whose shadows made all Europe honour him.

VALDES

Faustus, these books, thy wit, and our experience
Shall make all nations to canonize us.   120
As Indian Moors obey their Spanish lords,
So shall the subjects of every element
Be always serviceable to us three.
Like lions shall they guard us when we please,
Like Almaine rutters with their horsemen's staves,   125
Or Lapland giants trotting by our sides;

108   *three* either the three learned professions of law, medicine, and the Church or, more
      likely, the three divisions of human existence: body (the material world, *law and
      physic*); mind (*philosophy*); and soul (*divinity*)
112   *concise* brief and direct, not diffuse
      syllogisms in logic, an argument in which two propositions or premises that share
      a common term result in a third proposition or conclusion
113   *Gravelled* confounded
115   *problems* topics of academic debate
116   *Musaeus* Virgil (*Aeneid* vi, 667–8) describes this legendary, pre-Homeric poet sur-
      rounded by the spirits of priests and bards in the Elysian fields of the Greek underworld.
117   *Agrippa* The magician and necromancer Henry Cornelius Agrippa von Nettesheim
      (1486–1535), author of *De Occulta Philosophia* and *De Vanitate Scientiarum*, was
      famous for his reputed power of invoking shadows – spirits or spirit representations –
      of the dead.
120   *canonise* deify, with ironic echo of ecclesiastical canon law and of the enrolling or
      canonising of saints
121   *Indian Moors* American Indians
122   *subjects* A (spirits B) a) the substances of which material forms are made (*OED* 5),
      hence materialised spirits (see the shapes in Shakespeare's *Tempest*, III.ii.18), b)
      those subject to a lord; servants, retainers. As a necromancer, Faustus intends to
      rule all the elements through his power over their spirits.
125   'Like German cavalry with lances'
126   *Lapland giants* On another occasion Marlowe refers to the inhabitants of the polar regions
      in this way: 'tall and sturdy men, Giants as big as hugy Polypheme' (2 *Tamburlaine*,
      I.i.37–8).

Sometimes like women, or unwedded maids,
Shadowing more beauty in their airy brows
Than in the white breasts of the Queen of Love.
From Venice shall they drag huge argosies,   130
And from America the golden fleece
That yearly stuffs old Philip's treasury,
If learned Faustus will be resolute.

FAUSTUS

Valdes, as resolute am I in this
As thou to live, therefore object it not.   135

CORNELIUS

The miracles that magic will perform
Will make thee vow to study nothing else.
He that is grounded in astrology,
Enriched with tongues, well seen in minerals,
Hath all the principles magic doth require: 140
Then doubt not, Faustus, but to be renowned
And more frequented for this mystery,
Than heretofore the Delphian oracle.
The spirits tell me they can dry the sea,
And fetch the treasure of all foreign wrecks,   145
Ay, all the wealth that our forefathers hid

129 *in the* Greg (in their A; has the B)
130 *From* A2 (For A1)
       argosies rich merchant ships from Ragusa, near Venice, later poetically linked with
       the Argo, the mythical ship in which Jason sailed to search for the golden fleece
131 *golden fleece* a) 'treasure' – from the magical pelt sought by Jason and the Argonauts,
       b) a pun on 'fleece': strip, plunder. The enormous wealth plundered from America
       was also the object of English piratical attacks on Spanish ships. The other specifically
       Spanish and Catholic connotation of the phrase concerns the chivalric Order of the
       Golden Fleece, founded by Philip III, Duke of Burgundy, which had passed to the
       control of the Spanish Hapsburg monarchy.
132 *stuffs* A (stuff'd B) The change from present to past tense between texts suggests
       that the B-text manuscript post-dates the death of '*old Philip*', (Philip II of Spain
       1527–98).
135 *object it not* don't raise any objections
138 *grounded* well schooled
139 *tongues* Greek and Hebrew were desirable for those who would converse with spirits, but
       Latin was the recognized common language: 'Thou art a scholar: speak to it Horatio.'
       Hamlet, I.i.42.
       seen in minerals B (seen minerals A); knowledgeable about the properties of minerals
142 'more sought after for practising this art'
143 *Delphian oracle* the oracle of Apollo at Delphi

Within the massy entrails of the earth.
Then tell me, Faustus, what shall we three want?

FAUSTUS

Nothing Cornelius! O this cheers my soul!
Come, show me some demonstrations magical,   150
That I may conjure in some lusty grove,
And have these joys in full possession.

VALDES

Then haste thee to some solitary grove,
And bear wise Bacon's and Abanus' works,
The Hebrew Psalter, and New Testament;   155
And whatsoever else is requisite
We will inform thee ere our conference cease.

CORNELIUS

Valdes, first let him know the words of art,
And then, all other ceremonies learned,
Faustus may try his cunning by himself.   160

VALDES

First, I'll instruct thee in the rudiments,
And then wilt thou be perfecter than I.

FAUSTUS

Then come and dine with me, and after meat
We'll canvass every quiddity thereof:
For ere I sleep, I'll try what I can do.   165
This night I'll conjure, though I die therefore.

Exeunt

147 *massy* solid
151 *lusty* A1 (little A2, 3; bushy B); in the sixteenth century, the word could mean 'pleasant'
154 *wise Bacon's and Abanus' works* Roger Bacon (?1214–94), protagonist of Greene's
     Friar Bacon and Friar Bungay, was an Oxford philosopher popularly supposed to
     have dabbled in black magic. Abanus is perhaps Pietro d'Abano (?1250–1316), Italian
     humanist and physician, who was also believed to have been a conjuror. As well as
     the works of these two, which would supply formulae for incantation, Faustus would
     need certain Psalms (especially 22 and 51) and the opening words of St John's Gospel
     for his conjuring.
161 *rudiments* 'all that which is called vulgarly the vertue of worde, herbe, & stone: which
     is used by unlawful charmes, without natural causes . . . such kinde of charmes as
     commonlie daft wives use.' James I, *Daemonologie* (Edinburgh, 1597), p. 11
164 *canvass every quiddity* explore every detail; *quiddity* is a scholastic term denoting the
     essence of a thing, that which makes it what it is

[Scene 2]

Enter two SCHOLARS

1 SCHOLAR

I wonder what's become of Faustus, that was wont to make our
schools ring with *sic probo*.

2 SCHOLAR

That shall we know; for see, here comes his boy.

Enter WAGNER

1 SCHOLAR

How now sirra, where's thy master?

WAGNER

God in heaven knows.   5

2 SCHOLAR

Why, dost not thou know?

WAGNER

Yes I know, but that follows not.

1 SCHOLAR

Go to sirra, leave your jesting, and tell us where he is.

WAGNER

That follows not necessary by force of argument, that you, being
licentiate, should stand upon't; therefore acknowledge your error,   10
and be attentive.

2 SCHOLAR

Why, didst thou not say thou knew'st?

WAGNER

Have you any witness on't?

1 SCHOLAR

Yes sirra, I heard you.

WAGNER

Ask my fellow if I be a thief.   15

---

2   *sic probo* thus I prove it: a term from scholastic disputation
5   *God . . . knows* would normally imply that *only* God knows, but it does not logically
     follow that if God knows, Wagner does *not* know
10   *licentiate* licensed, i.e. a graduate allowed to progress to a higher degree, but also a
     pun on 'licensed man' (professional fool)
     stand upon't base yourself on that, i.e. think that that makes you wise
15   *Ask . . . thief* proverbial; *fellow* companion, friend

2 SCHOLAR

Well, you will not tell us.

WAGNER

Yes sir, I will tell you; yet if you were not dunces you would never
ask me such a question. For is not he *corpus naturale*? And is not
that *mobile*? Then wherefore should you ask me such a question?
But that I am by nature phlegmatic, slow to wrath, and prone to   20
lechery – to love I would say – it were not for you to come within
forty foot of the place of execution, although I do not doubt to
see you both hanged the next sessions. Thus having triumphed
over you, I will set my countenance like a precisian, and begin to
speak thus: Truly my dear brethren, my master is within at dinner   25
with Valdes and Cornelius, as this wine, if it could speak, it would
inform your worships. And so the Lord bless you, preserve you,
and keep you, my dear brethren, my dear brethren.   *Exit*

1 SCHOLAR

Nay then, I fear he is fallen into that damned art, for which they
two are infamous through the world.   30

2 SCHOLAR

Were he a stranger, and not allied to me, yet should I grieve for
him. But come, let us go and inform the Rector, and see if he by
his grave counsel can reclaim him.

1 SCHOLAR

O, but I fear me nothing can reclaim him.

2 SCHOLAR

Yet let us try what we can do.   35

Exeunt

17   *dunces* blockheads. The followers of Duns Scotus were commonly known as Dunses,
but here it is Wagner himself who indulges in the academic cavilling characteristic
of the Scotists.
18–19   *corpus naturale* a natural body
mobile capable of movement; changeable. According to Aristotelian physics, the
definitive property of a natural body is that it is subject to change.
20   *phlegmatic* In old physiology, there were four 'humours' that governed the body:
black bile (cold and dry, which caused 'melancholy'); yellow bile (hot and dry, which
caused 'choler'); blood (hot and wet, which caused 'sanguinity'); and phlegm, cold
and wet. A phlegmatic person is predisposed to indolence and sluggishness, but slow
to anger.
22   *place of execution* i.e. place where a formal act, or act of skill is being performed;
here, a gathering of necromancers at dinner, introducing the wordplay on *hanged*
(l. 23)
24   *precisian* puritan; Wagner now apes the unctuous speech of this sect
32   *Rector* head of the university

[Scene 3]

Enter FAUSTUS *to conjure*

FAUSTUS

Now that the gloomy shadow of the earth,
Longing to view Orion's drizzling look,
Leaps from th'antarctic world unto the sky,
And dims the welkin with her pitchy breath:
Faustus, begin thine incantations,   5
And try if devils will obey thy hest,
Seeing thou hast prayed and sacrificed to them.
Within this circle is Jehovah's name,
Forward and backward anagrammatized;
The breviated names of holy saints,   10
Figures of every adjunct to the heavens,

---

1 *shadow of the earth* In *The French Academic*, La Primaudaye explains that 'the night,
also, is no other thing than the shadow of the earth'. See also John Norton Smith,
'Marlowe's *Faustus*', *N & Q* NS 25 (1978), pp. 436–7.
2 *Orion's drizzling look* the rainy constellation of Orion
3 Marlowe seems to have thought that night advances from the southern hemisphere.
4 *welkin* sky
pitchy Pitch is a sticky substance obtained as a residue from the distillation of wood
tar and was used for protecting wood from moisture; hence 'pitchy' meant both
black and stinking.
7 *prayed and sacrificed* A period of prayer and sacrifice, a kind of spiritual preparation,
was a pre-requisite for conjuring.
8 *circle* Before he began his conjuring, the magician would draw a circle round himself,
inscribing on the periphery certain signs. So long as the circle was unbroken and the
magician stayed inside it, no evil spirit could harm him.
Jehovah a late medieval Hebrew word for God, combining the four Hebraic letters
representing the name Yahweh (meaning 'God', but never spoken aloud) with the
Hebraic vowels of Adonai (meaning 'lord'), the word commonly used to refer to
Him. Sixteenth-century magic was greatly influenced by the Jewish Cabbala (the
oral and sometimes later regarded as mystical tradition handed down from
Moses).
9 *anagrammatized* B (and agramathist A), made into an anagram
9–12 Faustus's conjuring is, ironically, a literary act, depending on the patterns and control
of spelling, rhetoric and grammar.
10 *breviated* A (Th'abbreviated B); shortened
11 *Figures* a) diagrams, b) tropes, rhetorical patterns
adjunct a) in grammar, anything added to expand on the subject, b) in logic, an
accompanying quality or circumstance added to the essence of a thing, c) hence, here,
any heavenly body joined to the firmament

17

And characters of signs and erring stars,
By which the spirits are enforced to rise.
Then fear not Faustus, but be resolute,
And try the uttermost magic can perform.   15
Sint mihi dei acherontis propitii. Valeat numen triplex Jehovae! Ignei,
aerii, aquatici, terreni spiritus salvete! Orientis princeps, Belzebub
inferni ardentis monarcha, et Demogorgon, propitiamus vos, ut
appareat et surgat Mephastophilis. Quid tu moraris? Per Jehovam,
Gehennam, et consecratam aquam quam nunc spargo; signumque   20
crucis quod nunc facio; et per vota nostra, ipse nunc surgat nobis
dicatus Mephastophilis.

Enter a DEVIL

I charge thee to return and change thy shape,
Thou art too ugly to attend on me;

12   *characters* symbols
     signs i.e. of the zodiac
     erring stars planets, because they appear to err (wander, from the Latin *errare*, 'to
     lead astray') across the sky
16–22 'May the gods of Acheron look favourably upon me. Away with the spirit of the three-
     fold Jehovah. Welcome, spirits of fire, air, water, and earth. We ask your favour, O
     Prince of the East, Belzebub (monarch of burning hell), and Demogorgon, that
     Mephastophilis may appear and rise. Why do you delay? By Jehovah, Gehenna, and
     the holy water which I now sprinkle, and the sign of the cross which I now form, and
     by our vows, may Mephastophilis himself now rise, compelled to obey us.'
       Rejecting the God of Heaven, the Christian God in Three Persons, Faustus turns
     to His infernal counterpart: *Acheron* is one of the rivers in the Greek underworld,
     Orientis princeps (the Prince of the East) is Lucifer (see Isaiah xiv, 12), and *Demogorgon*
     is, in classical mythology, one of the most terrible primeval gods. Faustus hails the
     spirits of the elements: 'they make them believe, that at the fall of Lucifer, some spirits
     fell in the aire, some in the fire, some in the water, some in the lande' (*Daemonologie*,
     p. 20). The name *Mephastophilis* was not, apparently, known before the Faust legend;
     this seems to have been Marlowe's preferred spelling – it is the one used most fre-
     quently in the A-text. The different spellings are discussed by William Empson in
     Faustus and the Censor, 1987.
       Many invocations to the devil express similar surprise and impatience at his delay,
     after which the conjuror redoubles his efforts. Gehenna, the valley of Hinnom, was
     a place of sacrifice. Dr Faustus seems now to be renouncing his Christian baptism,
     misusing the baptismal water and forswearing the vows made at his christening. In
     devil-worship, the sign of the cross had a double function: a powerful charm to
     overcome diabolic disobedience, it also protected the conjuror from injury by any
     spirit that might appear.
17   *terreni* Greg (*om* Qq); Faustus would invoke the spirits of all four elements
18   *Belzebub* Marlowe's form of the name has been retained because at certain points (e.g.
     5.12) this suits better with the metre than the more commonly used Hebraic Beelzebub.

Go and return an old Franciscan friar,   25
That holy shape becomes a devil best.   *Exit* DEVIL
I see there's virtue in my heavenly words!
Who would not be proficient in this art?
How pliant is this Mephastophilis,
Full of obedience and humility,   30
Such is the force of magic and my spells.
Now Faustus, thou art conjuror laureate
That canst command great Mephastophilis.
Quin redis, Mephastophilis, fratris imagine!

Enter MEPHASTOPHILIS [*disguised as a friar*]

MEPHASTOPHILIS
Now Faustus, what would'st thou have me do?   35
FAUSTUS
I charge thee wait upon me whilst I live,
To do what ever Faustus shall command,
Be it to make the moon drop from her sphere,
Or the ocean to overwhelm the world.
MEPHASTOPHILIS
I am a servant to great Lucifer,   40
And may not follow thee without his leave;
No more than he commands must we perform.
FAUSTUS
Did not he charge thee to appear to me?
MEPHASTOPHILIS
No, I came now hither of mine own accord.

19 *Quid tu moraris* Ellis (*quod tumeraris* Qq)
23 *change thy shape EFB* describes a creature of fire, which appears at this point and
    eventually takes the shape of a man; the B-text asks for a 'Dragon' in what seems to be
    an anticipatory stage direction, the woodcut on the B-text titlepage shows an emergent
    dragon on the ground beside the conjuror's circle, and an inventory of props belonging
    to the Admiral's men, dated 10 March 1598 records a 'dragon in fostes' (see Intro.
    p. xix). A wary magician always stipulated from the beginning that a pleasing shape
    should be assumed.
32 *laureate* The laurel wreath of excellence was given to poets in ancient Greece; see
    note 9–12 above.
34 'Why do you not return, Mephastophilis, in the likeness of a friar'
    redis Boas (*regis* A; this line, and the two preceding ones, are omitted in B)
38–9 *moon ... world* These powers are common amongst enchanters in classical literature;
    compare Prospero's speech in Shakespeare's *The Tempest*, V.i.41-50.
44 Kocher (p. 160) calls this the well-established 'doctrine of voluntary ascent'.

FAUSTUS
  Did not my conjuring speeches raise thee? Speak!
MEPHASTOPHILIS   45
  That was the cause, but yet *per accidens,*
  For when we hear one rack the name of God,
  Abjure the Scriptures, and his saviour Christ,
  We fly in hope to get his glorious soul,
  Nor will we come, unless he use such means
  Whereby he is in danger to be damned: 50
  Therefore the shortest cut for conjuring
  Is stoutly to abjure the Trinity,
  And pray devoutly to the prince of hell.
FAUSTUS
  So Faustus hath already done, and holds this principle:
  There is no chief but only Belzebub,   55
  To whom Faustus doth dedicate himself.
  This word damnation terrifies not him,
  For he confounds hell in Elysium:
  His ghost be with the old philosophers.
  But leaving these vain trifles of men's souls,   60
  Tell me, what is that Lucifer thy lord?
MEPHASTOPHILIS
  Arch-regent and commander of all spirits.
FAUSTUS
  Was not that Lucifer an angel once?

46 *per accidens* literally 'by accident'; in logic, not of the real essence of a thing, i.e. a surface reason, incidental to the real cause
47 *rack* torture, tear apart (i.e. by anagrammatising it), hence 'strain the meaning of words' (*OED* v 1.3)
49 *glorious* a) shining, b) boastful, vainglorious
53 *stoutly* arrogantly, stubbornly, uncompromisingly
59 *confounds hell in Elysium* makes no distinction between the Christian concept of hell and the pagan (Greek) notion of the after-life in Elysium. Marlowe has already coupled the two: 'Hell and Elysium swarm with ghosts of men' (*1 Tamburlaine,* V.ii.403). Nashe may be referring to either of these passages when he scorns the writers that 'thrust Elisium into hell' (Preface to Greene's *Menaphon* [1589], ed. McKerrow, iii, 316)
60 *old philosophers* those who shared his disbelief in an eternity of punishment; the line seems to come from a saying of Averroes, the Arab commentator on Aristotle: *sit anima mea cum philosophis* (cf. J. C. Maxwell, *N & Q,* cxiv [1949], pp. 334–5; J. M. Steadman, *N & Q,* ccvii [1962], pp. 327–9)
62–76 This question and answer dialogue on matters of belief is a parody of the Christian 'catechism' (a treatise for instruction in the principles of the Christian religion, in the form of question and answer).
64 *that Lucifer* A simple account of the history of Lucifer is given in Isaiah xiv, 12–15

MEPHASTOPHILIS
  Yes Faustus, and most dearly loved of God.
FAUSTUS   65
  How comes it then that he is prince of devils?
MEPHASTOPHILIS
  O, by aspiring pride and insolence,
  For which God threw him from the face of heaven.
FAUSTUS
  And what are you that live with Lucifer?
MEPHASTOPHILIS
  Unhappy spirits that fell with Lucifer,
  Conspired against our God with Lucifer,   70
  And are for ever damned with Lucifer.
FAUSTUS
  Where are you damned?
MEPHASTOPHILIS
  In hell.
FAUSTUS
  How comes it then that thou art out of hell?
MEPHASTOPHILIS   75
  Why this is hell, nor am I out of it.
  Think'st thou that I, who saw the face of God,
  And tasted the eternal joys of heaven,
  Am not tormented with ten thousand hells
  In being deprived of everlasting bliss?
  O Faustus, leave these frivolous demands,   80
  Which strike a terror to my fainting soul.

76–80 Caxton, while locating hell 'in the most lowest place, most derke, and most vyle of
       the erthe', stressed that it is a state as well as a place; the condemned sinner is like a
       man 'that had a grete maladye, so moche that he sholde deye, and that he were brought
       into a fair place and plesaunt for to have Joye and solace; of so moche shold he be
       more hevy and sorowful' (*The Mirrour of the World* [1480], ii, 18). Marlowe's concept
       of hell at this point may be compared with Milton's; like Mephastophilis, Satan
       cannot escape:
                    For within him Hell
         He brings, and round about him, nor from Hell
         One step, no more than from himself can fly
         By change of place.   *Paradise Lost*, iv, 20–23
       Mephastophilis' account of the torment of deprivation is translated from St John
       Chrysostom: *si decem mille gehennas quis dixerit, nihil tale est quale ab illa beata
       visione excidere* (see John Searle, *T.L.S.*, 15 February 1936).

21

FAUSTUS

What, is great Mephastophilis so passionate
For being deprived of the joys of heaven!
Learn thou of Faustus manly fortitude,
And scorn those joys thou never shalt possess.   85
Go bear these tidings to great Lucifer,
Seeing Faustus hath incurred eternal death
By desperate thoughts against Jove's deity:
Say, he surrenders up to him his soul
So he will spare him four and twenty years,   90
Letting him live in all voluptuousness,
Having thee ever to attend on me,
To give me whatsoever I shall ask,
To tell me whatsoever I demand,
To slay mine enemies, and aid my friends,   95
And always be obedient to my will.
Go, and return to mighty Lucifer,
And meet me in my study at midnight,
And then resolve me of thy master's mind.

MEPHASTOPHILIS   100

I will Faustus.   *Exit*

FAUSTUS

Had I as many souls as there be stars
I'd give them all for Mephastophilis.
By him I'll be great emperor of the world,
And make a bridge through the moving air
To pass the ocean with a band of men,   105
I'll join the hills that bind the Afric shore
And make that land continent to Spain
And both contributory to my crown –

83   *passionate* impassioned, swayed by strong feelings
87   *these* B (those A)
91   *So* on condition that
104–9   Both A- and B-texts punctuate very lightly here. Some modern editors add a semi-
        colon after 'men' (l. 106), but this interrupts the tumultuous association of word and
        idea whereby he imagines that by joining landmasses together a very small army
        could make him an emperor. Persian King Xerxes built a pontoon bridge across the
        Dardanelles to invade Greece. Alexander the Great (a figure who appears at 10.45–60)
        famously captured the island fortress of Tyre by joining it to the mainland with a
        1000 metre causeway.
107–8   The hills on either side of the Straits of Gibraltar would, if joined together, unite
        Africa and Europe into a single continent.

The emperor shall not live but by my leave,   110
Nor any potentate of Germany.
Now that I have obtained what I desire
I'll live in speculation of this art
Till Mephastophilis return again.   *Exit*

110–11   *emperor . . . Germany* The Holy Roman Emperor was elected by German princes. In
Faustus's time, the Emperor was Charles V, Duke of Burgundy, King of the Spanish
Empire (see l. 108), and ruler of Hapsburg lands in Austria/Hungary. Faustus wishes
to be Emperor of the entire world (l. 104).

[Scene 4]

Enter WAGNER *and the* CLOWN

WAGNER

Sirra boy, come hither.

CLOWN

How, boy? Zounds, boy! I hope you have seen many boys with
such pickadevants as I have. Boy, quotha!

WAGNER

Tell me sirra, hast thou any comings in?

CLOWN

Ay, and goings out too; you may see else.   5

WAGNER

Alas poor slave, see how poverty jesteth in his nakedness! The
villain is bare, and out of service, and so hungry, that I know he
would give his soul to the devil for a shoulder of mutton, though
it were blood raw.

CLOWN

How, my soul to the devil for a shoulder of mutton though 'twere   10
blood raw? Not so good friend; by'rlady, I had need have it well
roasted, and good sauce to it, if I pay so dear.

WAGNER

Well, wilt thou serve me, and I'll make thee go like *qui mihi
discipulus*?

CLOWN

How, in verse?   15

WAGNER

No sirra; in beaten silk and stavesacre.

Scene 4   The B-text version of this scene, which is greatly changed to accommodate different
comedians and an altered theatrical taste, is printed in the Appendix.
3   *pickadevants* small, pointed beards (Fr. *piqué devant*, pointed in front).
4   *comings in* earnings, income
5   *goings out* a) outgoings, expenses, b) the phrase becomes a visual joke ('see') if the
Clown pokes a finger through a hole in his clothes, or covers up a hole in mock
embarrassment.
6–9   *see . . . raw* The language here might encourage an actor mockingly to adopt the
tones of an evangelical preacher; compare 2.24–8.
7   *out of service* out of a job
13–14   *qui mihi discipulus* you who are my pupil: the opening words of a didactic Latin poem
by the schoolmaster William Lily which would be familiar to every Elizabethan schoolboy

24

CLOWN

How, how, knavesacre? Ay, I thought that was all the land his
father left him! Do ye hear, I would be sorry to rob you of your
living.

WAGNER

Sirra, I say in stavesacre. 20

CLOWN

Oho, oho, stavesacre! Why then belike, if I were your man, I should
be full of vermin.

WAGNER

So thou shalt, whether thou be'st with me or no. But sirra, leave
your jesting, and bind your self presently unto me for seven years,
or I'll turn all the lice about thee into familiars, and they shall tear 25
thee in pieces.

CLOWN

Do you hear sir? You may save that labour: they are too familiar
with me already – zounds, they are as bold with my flesh as if they
had paid for my meat and drink.

WAGNER

Well, do you hear sirra? Hold, take these guilders. 30

CLOWN

Gridirons; what be they?

16 *beaten silk* silk embroidered or with a woven pattern in gold or silver thread, but
    here signifying that, as Wagner's servant, he will be well beaten
    stavesacre powder made from seeds of delphinium (*delphinium staphisagria*) used
    to kill vermin
17–22 Deliberate mishearing is still a stock comedy routine, as is mixing an onstage
    conversation with direct address to the audience. The clown has been insulted by
    Wagner since his entrance. He turns the tables with the invented word 'knavesacre'
    by observing, probably to the audience but in such a manner that Wagner clearly
    hears the insult, that Wagner only inherited one acre from his father. (Compare
    'wiseacre', a contemptuous term for someone who thinks himself wise). He turns
    back to Wagner with the comment that the revenue ('living') from one acre would
    not be enough to pay wages. Wagner corrects the word, and the clown's repeated
    'oho' again allows him to draw in the audience before delivering the killer blow that
    any servant of Wagner's will be flea-ridden.
24 *presently* immediately
    seven years the standard period for indentured service or apprenticeship
25 *familiars* familiar spirits or devils, often taking the form of domestic animals
29 *paid . . . drink* (my A; their B) i.e. paid for his board (in order to fatten him up)
30 *guilders* Dutch gold or silver coins. Foreign coins were legal tender in England as
    long as they were of the correct weight, see Harrison's *Description of England* in
    Holinshed's *Chronicles* (1577, ii, 25).
31 *Gridirons* grids made of metal bars, used for cooking or as instruments of torture

WAGNER

Why, French crowns.

CLOWN

'Mass, but for the name of French crowns a man were as good
have as many English counters! And what should I do with these?

WAGNER

Why, now, sirra, thou art at an hour's warning whensoever or   35
wheresoever the devil shall fetch thee.

CLOWN

No, no, here take your gridirons again.

WAGNER

Truly I'll none of them.

CLOWN

Truly but you shall.

WAGNER

Bear witness I gave them him.   40

CLOWN

Bear witness I give them you again.

WAGNER

Well, I will cause two devils presently to fetch thee away. [*Calls*]
Baliol and Belcher!

CLOWN

Let your Baliol and your Belcher come here, and I'll knock them,
they were never so knocked since they were devils! Say I should   45
kill one of them, what would folks say? Do ye see yonder tall fellow

33 *'Mass* by the holy mass
34 *counters* worthless tokens, with pun on 'the Counter' (debtor's prison)
37–41 The business with the coins must be similar to that in scene viii of *The Taming of A
Shrew* where the Clown starts a sequence with 'Here, here, take your two shillings
again'. The actors draw the audience into their comic play to 'Bear witness'.
43 *Baliol* probably a corruption of 'Belial'; *Belcher* is also perhaps a mispronunciation
of 'Belzebub'
44–8 The Clown perhaps jokes on 'belly-all' and 'belch'. His lines depend for their humour
on the extended stage business they invite. He might act out the pummelling he
intends to give the devils and the kudos he will gain by beating them. A similar
passage occurs in *A Looking Glass for London* which was written by Lodge and Greene,
acted by Strange's Men in 1592, and printed in 1594. Here the Clown attacks the
devil who has come to carry him to hell; when the devil pleads that he is mortally
wounded, the Clown triumphs:

> Then may I count my selfe I thinke a tall man, that am able to kill a diuell. Now
> who dare deale with me in the parish, or what wench in *Ninivie* will not loue me,
> when they say, there goes he that beate the diuell.   (G3')

44 *knock* beat
46 *tall* fine

in the round slop, he has killed the devil! So I should be called
'Killdevil' all the parish over.

Enter two DEVILS, *and the* CLOWN *runs up
and down crying*

WAGNER
Baliol and Belcher, spirits, away!

Exeunt [DEVILS]

CLOWN
What, are they gone? A vengeance on them! They have vile long   50
nails. There was a he devil and a she devil. I'll tell you how you
shall know them: all he devils has horns, and all she devils has
clefts and cloven feet.

WAGNER
Well sirra, follow me.

CLOWN
But do you hear? If I should serve you, would you teach me to   55
raise up Banios and Belcheos?

WAGNER
I will teach thee to turn thy self to anything, to a dog, or a cat, or
a mouse, or a rat, or any thing.

CLOWN
How! A Christian fellow to a dog, or a cat, a mouse, or a rat? No,
no sir, if you turn me into anything, let it be in the likeness of a   60
little pretty frisking flea, that I may be here, and there, and every-
where. O I'll tickle the pretty wenches' plackets! I'll be amongst
them i'faith.

WAGNER
Well sirra, come.

CLOWN
But, do you hear Wagner . . . ?   65

WAGNER
Baliol and Belcher!

---

47 *round slop* baggy pants, stock garments for comic characters; compare *Damon and
    Pythias*, 1571, Scene 13.83–94
53 *clefts* slits, with sexual pun
61 *frisking flea* In the medieval 'Song of the Flea', the poet envies the flea because it has
    free access to all parts of his mistress's body
62 *plackets* openings at the top of skirts, which also allowed access to the separate pocket
    worn beneath (also sometimes termed a placket); with sexual connotations

CLOWN

O Lord I pray sir, let Banio and Belcher go sleep.

WAGNER

Villain, call me Master Wagner; and let thy left eye be diametarily
fixed upon my right heel, with *quasi vestigias nostras insistere.*

Exit

CLOWN

God forgive me, he speaks Dutch fustian! Well, I'll follow him, I'll   70
serve him; that's flat.   *Exit*

68 *diametarily* diametrically
69 *quasi vestigias nostras insistere* 'as it were tread in our footsteps'; the construction is
    false (for *vestigiis nostris),* but this may be intentional
70 *Dutch fustian* gibberish – double Dutch; *fustian* is a coarse cloth made of flax and
    cotton

[Scene 5]

Enter FAUSTUS *in his study*

FAUSTUS

Now Faustus, must thou needs be damned,
And canst thou not be saved.
What boots it then to think of God or heaven?
Away with such vain fancies and despair,
Despair in God, and trust in Belzebub.   5
Now go not backward: no, Faustus, be resolute;
Why waverest thou? O, something soundeth in mine ears:
'Abjure this magic, turn to God again'.
Ay, and Faustus will turn to God again.
To God? He loves thee not: 10
The god thou servest is thine own appetite
Wherein is fixed the love of Belzebub.
To him I'll build an altar and a church,
And offer luke-warm blood of new-born babes.

Enter GOOD ANGEL *and* EVIL [ANGEL]

GOOD ANGEL

Sweet Faustus, leave that execrable art.   15
FAUSTUS

Contrition, prayer, repentance: what of them?
GOOD ANGEL

O they are means to bring thee unto heaven.
EVIL ANGEL

Rather illusions, fruits of lunacy,
That makes men foolish that do trust them most.
GOOD ANGEL

Sweet Faustus, think of heaven, and heavenly things.   20
EVIL ANGEL

No Faustus, think of honour and of wealth.
                                        Exeunt [ANGELS]

FAUSTUS

Of wealth!

---

3 *boots it* good is it
21 *and of wealth* A2 (and wealth A1)

29

Why, the signory of Emden shall be mine
When Mephastophilis shall stand by me.
What god can hurt thee, Faustus? Thou art safe,   25
Cast no more doubts. Come Mephastophilis,
And bring glad tidings from great Lucifer.
Is't not midnight? Come Mephastophilis:
Veni veni Mephastophile.

Enter MEPHASTOPHILIS

Now tell, what says Lucifer thy lord?   30
MEPHASTOPHILIS
That I shall wait on Faustus whilst he lives,
So he will buy my service with his soul.
FAUSTUS
Already Faustus hath hazarded that for thee.
MEPHASTOPHILIS
But Faustus, thou must bequeath it solemnly,
And write a deed of gift with thine own blood,   35
For that security craves great Lucifer.
If thou deny it, I will back to hell.
FAUSTUS
Stay Mephastophilis, and tell me,
What good will my soul do thy lord?
MEPHASTOPHILIS
Enlarge his kingdom.   40
FAUSTUS
Is that the reason he tempts us thus?

23 *signory of Emden* governorship of Emden – a port on the mouth of the Ems, at this time
    trading extensively with England. This is a somewhat modest ambition for someone
    who has the devil's assistance.
27 *glad tidings* This is ironic: the angels announced 'glad tidings of great joy', to the
    shepherds at the birth of Christ (Luke ii, 10).
29 *Veni . . . Mephastophile* 'Come, O come Mephastophilis'; a blasphemous parody of
    'veni, veni Emmanuel (translated in the nineteenth century as the hymn 'O come,
    O come Emmanuel')
30 *tell, what* A (tell me what B), see 5.145 below.
31 *he lives* B (I live A)
32 *So* provided that
33 *hazarded* jeopardized
40 *Enlarge his kingdom* 'Satan's chiefest drift & main point that he aimeth at, is the
    inlargement of his own kingdom, by the eternall destruction of man in the life to
    come', James Mason, *The Anatomie of Sorcerie* (1612), p. 55.

MEPHASTOPHILIS
Solamen miseris socios habuisse doloris.
FAUSTUS
Have you any pain that torture others?
MEPHASTOPHILIS
As great as have the human souls of men.
But tell me Faustus, shall I have thy soul?   45
And I will be thy slave and wait on thee,
And give thee more than thou hast wit to ask.
FAUSTUS
Ay Mephastophilis, I give it thee.
MEPHASTOPHILIS
Then stab thine arm courageously,
And bind thy soul, that at some certain day   50
Great Lucifer may claim it as his own,
And then be thou as great as Lucifer.
FAUSTUS
Lo Mephastophilis, for love of thee,
I cut mine arm, and with my proper blood
Assure my soul to be great Lucifer's,   55
Chief lord and regent of perpetual night.
View here the blood that trickles from mine arm,
And let it be propitious for my wish.
MEPHASTOPHILIS
But Faustus, thou must write it
In manner of a deed of gift.   60
FAUSTUS
Ay, so I will; but Mephastophilis,
My blood congeals and I can write no more.
MEPHASTOPHILIS
I'll fetch thee fire to dissolve it straight.   *Exit*
FAUSTUS
What might the staying of my blood portend?

42 proverbial; 'it is a comfort to the wretched to have had companions in misery'
43 *torture* B (tortures A), i.e. Do you who torture others have any pain? The B-text modernises the grammar rather than making a correction, but also reads 'Why, have you any pain that torture other?'
50 *certain* specified, fixed
52 *great* a) powerful, b) proud, arrogant
54 *proper* own
58 *propitious* a) favourable, b) an acceptable and effective sacrifice, c) blasphemously recalling Christ's own propitiatory sacrifice for the salvation of mankind

31

Is it unwilling I should write this bill?   65
Why streams it not, that I may write afresh:
'Faustus gives to thee his soul'. ah, there it stayed!
Why should'st thou not? Is not thy soul thine own?
Then write again: 'Faustus gives to thee his soul'.

Enter MEPHASTOPHILIS *with a chafer of coals*

MEPHASTOPHILIS
Here's fire, come Faustus, set it on.   70
FAUSTUS
So, now the blood begins to clear again.
Now will I make an end immediately.
MEPHASTOPHILIS
O what will not I do to obtain his soul!
FAUSTUS
Consummatum est, this bill is ended,
And Faustus hath bequeathed his soul to Lucifer.   75
But what is this inscription on mine arm?
Homo fuge. Whither should I fly?
If unto God, he'll throw thee down to hell;
My senses are deceived, here's nothing writ;
I see it plain, here in this place is writ,   80
Homo fuge! Yet shall not Faustus fly.
MEPHASTOPHILIS
I'll fetch him somewhat to delight his mind.   *Exit*

Enter [*again*] *with* DEVILS, *giving crowns and rich
apparel to* FAUSTUS; *and dance, and then depart*

65   *bill* written document
66   *streams* This word anticipates 13.68.
69   s.d. *chafer* usually a warming dish containing hot water (the source has 'dish of water'). A dish of burning coals is more redolent of hell.
70   *set it on* 'set his blood in a saucer on warm ashes' *EFB*, vi
71   Greg observes that no earthly fire will liquefy congealed blood
74   *Consummatum est* 'It is completed'; the last words of Christ on the cross: St John xix, 30
77–8 Compare Psalms cxxxix, 7–8 'Whither shall I go from thy spirit? Or whither shall I flee from thy presence? If I ascend into heaven, thou art there: if I lie down in hell, thou art there.'
77   *Homo fuge* Fly, O man

FAUSTUS

Speak Mephastophilis, what means this show?

MEPHASTOPHILIS

Nothing Faustus, but to delight thy mind withal,
And to show thee what magic can perform.   85

FAUSTUS

But may I raise up spirits when I please?

MEPHASTOPHILIS

Ay Faustus, and do greater things than these.

FAUSTUS

Then there's enough for a thousand souls!
Here Mephastophilis, receive this scroll,
A deed of gift of body and of soul: 90
But yet conditionally, that thou perform
All articles prescribed between us both.

MEPHASTOPHILIS

Faustus, I swear by hell and Lucifer
To effect all promises between us made.

FAUSTUS

Then hear me read them. On these conditions following: 95
First, that Faustus may be a spirit in form and substance.
Secondly, that Mephastophilis shall be his servant, and at his
command.
Thirdly, that Mephastophilis shall do for him, and bring him
whatsoever.   100
Fourthly, that he shall be in his chamber or house invisible.
Lastly, that he shall appear to the said John Faustus at all times, in
what form or shape soever he please.
I, John Faustus of Wittenberg, doctor, by these presents, do give
both body and soul to Lucifer, Prince of the East, and his minister   105
Mephastophilis; and furthermore grant unto them that, four and
twenty years being expired, the articles above written inviolate, full

---

96   *may* This permissive verb (in contrast to the 'shall' governing Mephastophilis's part
      in this contract) suggests that Faustus sees his spirit status as something to be put
      on and put off again as he pleases.
      a spirit A spirit, to the Elizabethans, was usually an evil one – a devil (see Shake-
      speare, Sonnet CXLIV); according to some theologians, who followed Aquinas, God
      could have no mercy on a devil who was *ipso facto* incapable of repenting. Compare
      7.11–17.
101   *he* i.e. Mephastophilis
104   *these presents* the legal articles

power to fetch or carry the said John Faustus, body and soul, flesh,
blood, or goods, into their habitation wheresoever.

By me John Faustus.   110

MEPHASTOPHILIS
Speak Faustus, do you deliver this as your deed?

FAUSTUS
Ay, take it; and the devil give thee good on't.

MEPHASTOPHILIS
Now Faustus, ask what thou wilt.

FAUSTUS
First will I question with thee about hell:
Tell me, where is the place that men call hell?   115

MEPHASTOPHILIS
Under the heavens.

FAUSTUS
Ay, but whereabout?

MEPHASTOPHILIS
Within the bowels of these elements,
Where we are tortured and remain for ever.
Hell hath no limits, nor is circumscribed   120
In one self place; for where we are is hell,
And where hell is, must we ever be.
And to conclude, when all the world dissolves,
And every creature shall be purified,
All places shall be hell that is not heaven.   125

FAUSTUS
Come, I think hell's a fable.

MEPHASTOPHILIS
Ay, think so still, till experience change thy mind.

FAUSTUS
Why? thinkst thou then that Faustus shall be damned?

MEPHASTOPHILIS
Ay, of necessity, for here's the scroll
Wherein thou hast given thy soul to Lucifer.   130

FAUSTUS
Ay, and body too; but what of that?
Think'st thou that Faustus is so fond to imagine

---

118   *these elements* the four elements (fire, air, earth, and water) below the sphere of the
      moon
121   *one self place* one particular place
132   *fond* foolish

That after this life there is any pain?

Tush, these are trifles and mere old wives' tales.

MEPHASTOPHILIS

But Faustus, I am an instance to prove the contrary;   135

For I am damned, and am now in hell.

FAUSTUS

How, now in hell? Nay, and this be hell, I'll willingly be damned

here! What, walking, disputing, etc ... But leaving off this, let me

have a wife, the fairest maid in Germany, for I am wanton and

lascivious, and cannot live without a wife.   140

MEPHASTOPHILIS

How, a wife? I prithee Faustus, talk not of a wife.

FAUSTUS

Nay sweet Mephastophilis, fetch me one, for I will have one.

MEPHASTOPHILIS

Well, thou wilt have one; sit there till I come.

I'll fetch thee a wife in the devil's name.   [*Exit*]

Enter [again] with a DEVIL *dressed like a woman,*
with fireworks

MEPHASTOPHILIS

Tell Faustus, how dost thou like thy wife?   145

FAUSTUS

A plague on her for a hot whore!

MEPHASTOPHILIS

Tut Faustus, marriage is but a ceremonial toy;

[*Exit* DEVIL]

If thou lovest me, think no more of it.

I'll cull thee out the fairest courtesans,

And bring them every morning to thy bed: 150

She whom thine eye shall like, thy heart shall have,

Be she as chaste as was Penelope,

133 *after ... pain* Compare Lucretius's poem *De Rerum Natura,* a triumphant hymn on
     the mortality of the soul, and hence the impossibility of punishment after death.
138 *disputing* According to Chorus 1.18, this is Faustus's 'sweet delight'.
141 Mephastophilis is alarmed at this talk of marriage – which, in Christian terms, is
     considered a holy sacrament that saves sex between the partners from the sin of
     lechery.
147 *ceremonial toy* trifling ceremony
148 *think no more* B (think more A)
149 *cull* pick
152 *Penelope* wife of Ulysses, renowned for her fidelity to an absent husband

As wise as Saba, or as beautiful
As was bright Lucifer before his fall.
Hold, take this book, peruse it thoroughly. 155
The iterating of these lines brings gold;
The framing of this circle on the ground
Brings whirlwinds, tempests, thunder and lightning.
Pronounce this thrice devoutly to thy self,
And men in armour shall appear to thee, 160
Ready to execute what thou desir'st.

FAUSTUS

Thanks Mephastophilis, yet fain would I have a book wherein I
might behold all spells and incantations, that I might raise up
spirits when I please.

MEPHASTOPHILIS

Here they are in this book. *There turn to them* 165

FAUSTUS

Now would I have a book where I might see all characters and
planets of the heavens, that I might know their motions and
dispositions.

MEPHASTOPHILIS

Here they are too. *Turn to them*

FAUSTUS

Nay, let me have one book more, and then I have done, wherein 170
I might see all plants, herbs and trees that grow upon the earth.

MEPHASTOPHILIS

Here they be.

FAUSTUS

O thou art deceived!

MEPHASTOPHILIS

Tut, I warrant thee. *Turn to them*
[Exeunt]

---

153   *Saba* the Queen of Sheba, who confronted Solomon with 'hard questions', 1 Kings x
156   *iterating* repeating over and over
       lines a) verbal phrases, b) symbols
166   *characters* symbols
167   *motions* movements
168   *dispositions* a) positions relative to each other, b) nature of planets relative to their supposed effects
173   It seems that the sum total of the knowledge for which Faustus has sold his soul can be contained in one book. No wonder he is dismayed.
174   s.d. If Faustus is at his desk in the upstage 'discovery' space, Mephastophilis coud draw the curtain to hide them both. (See pp. xxii–xxiii.)

[Scene 6]

Enter ROBIN *the ostler with a book in his hand*

ROBIN
O this is admirable! Here I ha' stolen one of Doctor Faustus'
conjuring books, and i'faith I mean to search some circles for my
own use: now will I make all the maidens in our parish dance at
my pleasure stark naked before me, and so by that means I shall
see more than ere I felt, or saw yet.   5

Enter RAFE *calling* ROBIN

RAFE
Robin, prithee come away, there's a gentleman tarries to have his
horse, and he would have his things rubbed and made clean. He
keeps such a chafing with my mistress about it, and she has sent
me to look thee out. Prithee, come away.

ROBIN
Keep out, keep out; or else you are blown up, you are dismem-   10
bered, Rafe. Keep out, for I am about a roaring piece of work.

RAFE
Come, what dost thou with that same book? Thou canst not read!

ROBIN
Yes, my master and mistress shall find that I can read – he for his
forehead, she for her private study. She's born to bear with me, or
else my art fails.   15

RAFE
Why Robin, what book is that?

Scene 6 In the A-text the two episodes with Robin and Rafe are presented as a single scene; see
Introduction, p. xxii–xxiii. This revised edition follows Bevington and Rasmussen in
inserting the first Rafe and Robin scene at this point; Appendix 6 prints the B-text.
   0 *ostler* stable lad, groom
   2 *search* examine, probe
       circles magicians' circles; but the sexual overtones are obvious
   5 *ere* either 'previously' (archaic in Marlowe's time, and therefore perhaps chosen as
       a characteristic of Robin's speech) or 'ever'.
   8 *chafing* a) scolding, b) rubbing
  11 *roaring* dangerous
  14 *forehead* referring to cuckold's horns
       private study punning on 'private parts'
       bear with me a) put up with me, b) support my weight during sexual intercourse, c)
       bear my children

ROBIN

What book? Why the most intolerable book for conjuring that ere was invented by any brimstone devil.

RAFE

Canst thou conjure with it?

ROBIN

I can do all these things easily with it: first, I can make thee drunk   20
with 'ipocrase at any tavern in Europe for nothing, that's one of
my conjuring works.

RAFE

Our master parson says that's nothing.

ROBIN

True Rafe! And more, Rafe, if thou hast any mind to Nan Spit, our
kitchen-maid, then turn her and wind her to thy own use, as often   25
as thou wilt, and at midnight.

RAFE

O brave Robin! Shall I have Nan Spit, and to mine own use? On
that condition I'll feed thy devil with horsebread as long as he
lives, of free cost.

ROBIN

No more, sweet Rafe; let's go and make clean our boots which lie   30
foul upon our hands, and then to our conjuring in the devil's name.

Exeunt

17   *intolerable* unbearable, playing on 'bear with me', but Robin probably means 'incom-
     parable'
18   *brimstone* common name for sulphur, often used medicinally and as a fumigant, but
     its stinking odour is associated with the fumes of hell
21   *'ipocrase* hippocras – a spiced wine
28   *horsebread* fodder for horses
29   *of free cost* free of charge

[Scene 7]

[*Enter* FAUSTUS *and* MEPHASTOPHILIS]

FAUSTUS

When I behold the heavens, then I repent,
And curse thee, wicked Mephastophilis,
Because thou hast deprived me of those joys.

MEPHASTOPHILIS

Why Faustus,
Think'st thou heaven is such a glorious thing?   5
I tell thee 'tis not half so fair as thou,
Or any man that breathes on earth.

FAUSTUS

How provest thou that?

MEPHASTOPHILIS

It was made for man, therefore is man more excellent.

FAUSTUS

If it were made for man, 'twas made for me: 10
I will renounce this magic, and repent.

Enter GOOD ANGEL *and* EVIL ANGEL

GOOD ANGEL

Faustus, repent yet, God will pity thee.

EVIL ANGEL

Thou art a spirit, God cannot pity thee.

FAUSTUS

Who buzzeth in mine ears I am a spirit?
Be I a devil, yet God may pity me.   15
Ay, God will pity me if I repent.

EVIL ANGEL

Ay, but Faustus never shall repent.

Exeunt [ANGELS]

FAUSTUS

My heart's so hardened I cannot repent!

0   s.d. This ed. See 5.174 s.d.
12 *repent yet* A (repent, yet B) i.e. repent even now, while there is still time
14 *buzzeth* whispers
15 *Be I* This could mean either 'Even if I am', or else 'Even though I were'
18 Hardness (also called blindness) of heart is recognized as a very complex spiritual
     condition; the Litany of the Book of Common Prayer offers a special supplication:
     'From all blindness of heart . . . Good Lord, deliver us'. See Introduction, p. xiii.

Scarce can I name salvation, faith, or heaven,
But fearful echoes thunders in mine ears, 20
'Faustus, thou art damned'; then swords and knives,
Poison, guns, halters, and envenomed steel,
Are laid before me to dispatch myself:
And long ere this I should have slain myself,
Had not sweet pleasure conquered deep despair. 25
Have not I made blind Homer sing to me
Of Alexander's love, and Oenon's death?
And hath not he that built the walls of Thebes
With ravishing sound of his melodious harp,
Made music with my Mephastophilis? 30
Why should I die then, or basely despair?
I am resolved Faustus shall ne'er repent.
Come Mephastophilis, let us dispute again,
And argue of divine astrology.
Tell me, are there many heavens above the moon? 35

22   *halters* hangman's ropes
26   *blind Homer* The Greek poet was traditionally held to be blind
27   *Alexander . . . death* Alexander (Homer's name for Paris, son of Priam) fell in love
      with Oenone before he encountered Helen. After he was wounded in the Trojan War,
      he was carried to Oenone and died at her feet, whereupon she stabbed herself.
28–9 At the sound of Amphion's harp the stones were so affected that they rose of their
      own accord to form the walls of Thebes.
33–63 Faustus is both locked into his scholastic approach to knowledge through rhetorical
      disputation (7.33) and simultaneously hoping that Mephastophilis will give him
      hard information inaccessible to that method. His most urgent concern is to establish
      the structure of the universe. He briefly wonders whether the entire universe is not
      a single entity (7.37), but Mephastophilis swiftly returns him to the old Ptolemaic
      system, which taught that the earth is surrounded by a series of concentric chrystalline
      spheres. Each of the first seven spheres holds the orbit round the earth of one of the
      heavenly bodies (Moon, Mercury, Venus, Sun, Mars, Jupiter, Saturn). Beyond these
      is the sphere of the fixed stars, sometimes considered to include the *primum mobile*,
      the first mover, which imparts movement to the rest. The early church fathers
      postulated a further immoveable sphere, the *empyreal heaven* (7.58), which was the
      abode of God, and which shone with a piercing stainless light. Milton describes
      a similar cosmology in *Paradise Lost* when he identifies 'the planets seven'; 'the
      fixed'; 'And that crystalline sphere . . . that first moved' (III, 481-3). Unfortunately,
      Mephastophilis's replies to Faustus's questions comprise a miscellaneous jumble of
      commonly received knowledge, as Faustus himself points out (7.49; 53-4).
35–43 *Tell me . . . erring stars* Faustus asks first for confirmation of the number of spheres
      beyond the Moon, and whether in fact these do form a single ball. Mephastophilis
      replies that just as the four elements enclose each other (earth is surrounded by
      water, water by air, and air by fire), so each sphere or heaven is circled round by the

Arc all celestial bodies but one globe,
As is the substance of this centric earth?

MEPHASTOPHILIS

As are the elements, such are the spheres,
Mutually folded in each other's orb.
And, Faustus, all jointly move upon one axletree   40
Whose termine is termed the world's wide pole,
Nor are the names of Saturn, Mars, or Jupiter,
Feigned, but are erring stars.

FAUSTUS

But tell me, have they all one motion, both *situ et tempore*?

MEPHASTOPHILIS

All jointly move from east to west in four-and-twenty hours upon   45
the poles of the world, but differ in their motion upon the poles
of the zodiac.

FAUSTUS

Tush, these slender trifles Wagner can decide!
Hath Mephastophilis no greater skill?
Who knows not the double motion of the planets?   50
The first is finished in a natural day, the second thus: as Saturn in
thirty years; Jupiter in twelve; Mars in four; the Sun, Venus, and
Mercury in a year; the Moon in eight-and-twenty days. Tush, these
are freshmen's suppositions. But tell me, hath every sphere a
dominion or *intelligentia*?   55

ones beyond it, and all rotate upon a single axletree. Saturn, Mars, and the other
planets are individually recognizable: they are called *erring* or wandering stars to
distinguish them from the fixed stars which are joined to the firmament.

41   *termine* boundary (astronomical)

44   *situ et tempore* in direction and time

44–53   *all . . . days* When the movement of the planets is observed from earth, the planets
appear to move from east to west across the earth every night. But on successive nights
it seems as if they are moving from west to east relative to the positions of the zodiacal
constellations. This is the double motion (7.50) of the planets. Occasionally movement
relative to the constellations is reversed, a phenomenon known as the retrograde
motion of the planets. The complete revolution of each planet relative to the constellations is variable: Saturn 29½ years; Jupiter 11¾ years; Mars 1 year 11 months; Venus
7½ months and Mercury 3 months. Caxton (*Mirrour of the World* [1480], 1.13)
explains that each planet is like a fly crawling on a wheel: if the fly crawls in one
direction and the wheel turns in the opposite, the fly may be said to have two motions.

54   *freshmen's suppositions* elementary facts given to first-year undergraduates for them
to build an argument upon

54–5   *hath . . . intelligentia* The next question at issue relates to a theory first propounded
by Plato and developed in the Middle Ages, that each planet was guided by an angelic
spirit, commonly called the *intelligence*.

MEPHASTOPHILIS

Ay.

FAUSTUS

How many heavens or spheres are there?

MEPHASTOPHILIS

Nine: the seven planets, the firmament, and the empyreal heaven.

FAUSTUS

Well, resolve me in this question: why have we not conjunctions, oppositions, aspects, eclipses, all at one time, but in some years 60 we have more, in some less?

MEPHASTOPHILIS

Per inaequalem motum respectu totius.

FAUSTUS

Well, I am answered. Tell me who made the world?

MEPHASTOPHILIS

I will not.

FAUSTUS

Sweet Mephastophilis, tell me. 65

MEPHASTOPHILIS

Move me not, for I will not tell thee.

Let mans Soule be a Spheare, and then, in this,
The intelligence that moves, devotion is.
Donne, 'Good Friday, Riding Westwards'

Mephastophilis affirms the *intelligence,* but the theory was never really accepted by scientists.

59–62 *resolve me ... totius* Mephastophilis' answer to the next question sounds like a quotation from some astronomical textbook. Faustus asks about the behaviour of the planets, using technical but well-known astronomical terms; *conjunctions* are the apparent joinings together of two planets, whilst *oppositions* describes their relationships when most remote:

Therefore the love which us doth bind,
But Fate so enviously debars,
Is the Conjunction of the Mind,
And Opposition of the Stars.
Marvell, 'The Definition of Love'

Any position between the two extremes of conjunction and opposition was termed an *aspect.* To astrologers the differing situations and relations of the planets all have some particular significance – hence the horoscope. Faustus is finally told what he already knows: that the heavenly bodies do not all move at the same speed, and that for this reason ('through an irregular motion so far as the whole is concerned', l. 62) there are more eclipses etc. in some years than in others.

62 'Because of their unequal motion in respect of the whole'

66 *Move me not* Don't make me angry

FAUSTUS
    Villain, have I not bound thee to tell me anything?
MEPHASTOPHILIS
    Ay, that is not against our kingdom; but this is.
    Think thou on hell Faustus, for thou art damned.
FAUSTUS
    Think, Faustus, upon God, that made the world.   70
MEPHASTOPHILIS
    Remember this.   *Exit*
FAUSTUS
    Ay, go accursed spirit, to ugly hell,
    'Tis thou hast damned distressed Faustus' soul:
    Is't not too late?

            Enter GOOD ANGEL *and* EVIL [ANGEL]

EVIL ANGEL
    Too late.   75
GOOD ANGEL
    Never too late, if Faustus can repent.
EVIL ANGEL
    If thou repent, devils shall tear thee in pieces.
GOOD ANGEL
    Repent, and they shall never rase thy skin.
                                          Exeunt [ANGELS]
FAUSTUS
    Ah Christ my Saviour, seek to save
    Distressed Faustus' soul.   80

        Enter LUCIFER, BELZEBUB *and* MEPHASTOPHILIS

LUCIFER
    Christ cannot save thy soul, for he is just.
    There's none but I have interest in the same.
FAUSTUS
    O who art thou that look'st so terrible?
LUCIFER
    I am Lucifer, and this is my companion prince in hell.

    78   *rase* graze
    82   *interest* a) legal claim, b) financial interest; sin is sometimes spoken of as a debt that
          is redeemed by Christ's sacrifice

                                    43

FAUSTUS

O Faustus, they are come to fetch away thy soul! 85

LUCIFER

We come to tell thee thou dost injure us.
Thou talk'st of Christ, contrary to thy promise.
Thou should'st not think of God; think of the devil,
And of his dame too.

FAUSTUS

Nor will I henceforth: pardon me in this, 90
And Faustus vows never to look to heaven,
Never to name God, or to pray to him,
To burn his Scriptures, slay his ministers,
And make my spirits pull his churches down.

LUCIFER

Do so, and we will highly gratify thee. Faustus, we are come from 95
hell to show thee some pastime; sit down, and thou shalt see all
the Seven Deadly Sins appear in their proper shapes.

FAUSTUS

That sight will be as pleasing unto me, as Paradise was to Adam,
the first day of his creation.

LUCIFER

Talk not of Paradise, nor creation, but mark this show; talk of the 100
devil and nothing else. Come away.

Enter the SEVEN DEADLY SINS

Now Faustus, examine them of their several names and dispositions.

FAUSTUS

What art thou, the first?

PRIDE

I am Pride: I disdain to have any parents. I am like to Ovid's flea,
I can creep into every corner of a wench: sometimes like a periwig, 105
I sit upon her brow; or like a fan of feathers, I kiss her lips. Indeed
I do – what do I not! But fie, what a scent is here? I'll not speak
another word, except the ground were perfumed and covered with
cloth of arras.

89 *dame* old woman, wife, housewife, mother
97 *proper* own
102 *several* different, various
104 *Ovid's flea* The poet of 'Song of the Flea' (probably medieval but attributed to Ovid)
envies the flea for its freedom of movement over his mistress' body (see 4.61n).
108 *except* unless

FAUSTUS

What are thou, the second?   110

COVETOUSNESS

I am Covetousness, begotten of an old churl in an old leathern
bag: and might I have my wish, I would desire that this house, and
all the people in it, were turned to gold, that I might lock you up
in my good chest. O my sweet gold!

FAUSTUS

What art thou, the third?   115

WRATH

I am Wrath. I had neither father nor mother: I leaped out of a lion's
mouth when I was scarce half an hour old, and ever since I have
run up and down the world, with this case of rapiers, wounding
myself when I had nobody to fight withal. I was born in hell – and
look to it, for some of you shall be my father.   120

FAUSTUS

What art thou, the fourth?

ENVY

I am Envy, begotten of a chimney-sweeper, and an oyster- wife. I
cannot read, and therefore wish all books were burnt; I am lean
with seeing others eat – O that there would come a famine through
all the world, that all might die, and I live alone; then thou should'st   125
see how fat I would be! But must thou sit and I stand? Come down,
with a vengeance.

FAUSTUS

Away, envious rascal! What art thou, the fifth?

GLUTTONY

Who, I sir? I am Gluttony. My parents are all dead, and the devil
a penny they have left me but a bare pension, and that is thirty   130
meals a day and ten bevers – a small trifle to suffice nature. O, I
come of a royal parentage: my grandfather was a gammon of
bacon, my grandmother a hogshead of claret wine; my godfathers

---

109   *cloth of arras* tapestry; expensive, woven, pictorial wall-hangings originally from
         Arras in northern France
111–12   *leathern bag* the miser's purse
   118   *case* pair
   120   *some of you* Wrath addresses the audience
   122   *begotten . . . wife* Envy is filthy, and stinks
   131   *bevers* a) drinks, b) snacks, light meals
   133   *hogshead* a barrel containing sixty-three gallons

were these: Peter Pickle-Herring, and Martin Martlemas-Beef.
O, but my godmother! She was a jolly gentlewoman, and well-   135
beloved in every good town and city, her name was Mistress
Margery March-Beer. Now, Faustus, thou hast heard all my
progeny; wilt thou bid me to supper?

FAUSTUS

Ho, I'll see thee hanged; thou wilt eat up all my victuals.

GLUTTONY

Then the devil choke thee!   140

FAUSTUS

Choke thyself, Glutton. What art thou, the sixth?

SLOTH

I am Sloth; I was begotten on a sunny bank, where I have lain ever
since – and you have done me great injury to bring me from
thence. Let me be carried thither again by Gluttony and Lechery.
I'll not speak another word for a king's ransom.   145

FAUSTUS

What are you Mistress Minx, the seventh and last?

LECHERY

Who, I, sir? I am one that loves an inch of raw mutton better than
an ell of fried stockfish; and the first letter of my name begins with
Lechery.

LUCIFER

Away! To hell, to hell!   150

Exeunt the [SEVEN DEADLY] SINS

Now Faustus, how dost thou like this?

FAUSTUS

O this feeds my soul.

---

134   *Peter Pickle-Herring* a fat, buffoon figure, popular at the beginning of the seventeenth
century on the stage and in carnival celebrations in Holland and Germany, where
they regarded him as of English origin. Salty pickled herring, a food to be eaten
during Lent, was also provided in taverns (as are modern salted snacks) to promote
drinking.
Martlemas-Beef Meat, salted to preserve it for winter, was hung up around Martinmas
(11 November).

137   *March-Beer* a rich ale, made in March and left to mature for at least two years

138   *progeny* lineage (obsolete)

147–9 *I am one . . . Lechery* The words are rather obscure, but their sense is clear. Lechery prefers
a small quantity of virility to a large extent of impotence: *stockfish*, a long strip of dried
cod, is a common term of abuse, indicating impotence: 'he was begot between two
stockfishes', *Measure for Measure*, III.ii.98. The 'Minx' ends with a common form of
jest: cf. 'Her name begins with Mistress Purge', Middleton, *The Family of Love*, II.iii.53.

LUCIFER
Tut Faustus, in hell is all manner of delight.

FAUSTUS
O might I see hell, and return again, how happy were I then!

LUCIFER
Thou shalt; I will send for thee at midnight. In meantime, take   155
this book, peruse it thoroughly, and thou shalt turn thyself into
what shape thou wilt.

FAUSTUS
Great thanks, mighty Lucifer; this will I keep as chary as my life.

LUCIFER
Farewell, Faustus; and think on the devil.

FAUSTUS
Farewell, great Lucifer; come Mephastophilis.   160

Exeunt omnes

158   *chary* carefully

[Chorus 2]

WAGNER

Learned Faustus,
To know the secrets of astronomy
Graven in the book of Jove's high firmament,
Did mount himself to scale Olympus' top,
Being seated in a chariot burning bright,   5
Drawn by the strength of yoky dragons' necks.
He now is gone to prove cosmography,
And, as I guess, will first arrive at Rome,
To see the pope, and manner of his court,
And take some part of holy Peter's feast,   10
That to this day is highly solemnized.   *Exit* WAGNER

---

0 s.d. *Enter Wagner solus* This Chorus-like speech is given to Wagner in both the A-
  and B-texts, see Chorus 1 notes 0 and 28.
  solus alone
3 *Graven* carved, engraved
4 *Olympus* Mount Olympus was the home of the gods of Greek mythology.
6 *yoky dragons' necks* A (*yoaked* B) i.e. two dragons, the fiercest of mythical beasts, have
  taken on the attributes of a pair of domesticated animals, acting as one (as if joined
  with a yoke, or perhaps with their necks curved like yokes under the strain) and
  subjected to a man's will. This is the first recorded instance of the word in *OED*.
7 *prove* put to the test
  cosmography The art of describing and making maps of the universe, including the
  heavens and the earth, and combining astronomy, geography and history. The B-text
  adds a line explaining that this 'measures costs, and kingdomes of the earth'.
10 *holy Peter's feast* St Peter's feast day is 29 June

48

[Scene 8]

Enter FAUSTUS *and* MEPHASTOPHILIS

FAUSTUS
Having now, my good Mephastophilis,
Passed with delight the stately town of Trier,
Environed round with airy mountain tops,
With walls of flint, and deep entrenched lakes,
Not to be won by any conquering prince;   5
From Paris next, coasting the realm of France,
We saw the river Main fall into Rhine,
Whose banks are set with groves of fruitful vines;
Then up to Naples, rich Campania,
Whose buildings fair and gorgeous to the eye,   10
The streets straight forth, and paved with finest brick,
Quarters the town in four equivalents;
There saw we learned Maro's golden tomb,
The way he cut an English mile in length
Thorough a rock of stone in one night's space.   15
From thence to Venice, Padua – and the rest –
In midst of which a sumptuous temple stands,
That threats the stars with her aspiring top.
Thus hitherto hath Faustus spent his time.
But tell me now, what resting place is this?   20
Hast thou, as erst I did command,
Conducted me within the walls of Rome?

2 *Trier* Treves, in West Germany
6 *coasting* skirting
9 *Campania* Naples lies within the region of Campania
13 *learned Maro* The poet Virgil (Publius Virgilius Maro) was buried in Naples in 19
    B.C., and posthumously acquired some reputation as a magician. His tomb stands
    at the end of the promontory of Posilippo between Naples and Pozzuoli; legend
    ascribes the tunnel running through this promontory to his magic art.
16-18 *Venice . . . top EFB* lists very many more places and buildings on Faustus's tour of
    the world than are mentioned here, hence perhaps the vagueness of the A-text's *and
    the rest* (8.16). This is printed here within dashes since the *aspiring top* (8.18) must
    refer to the striking silhouette of the Basilica of St Anthony in Padua; *EFB* (p. 35)
    justifiably describes its 'pinnacles' as unique in Christendom. The B-text prints
    'Venice, Padua, and the East' and adds a quotation from the *EFB* description of St
    Mark's in Venice.
21 *erst* earlier

49

MEPHASTOPHILIS

   Faustus, I have; and because we will not be unprovided, I have

   taken up his holiness' privy chamber for our use.

FAUSTUS

   I hope his holiness will bid us welcome.   25

MEPHASTOPHILIS

   Tut, 'tis no matter man, we'll be bold with his good cheer.

   And now, my Faustus, that thou may'st perceive

   What Rome containeth to delight thee with,

   Know that this city stands upon seven hills

   That underprop the groundwork of the same;   30

   Just through the midst runs flowing Tiber's stream,

   With winding banks, that cut it in two parts;

   Over the which four stately bridges lean,

   That makes safe passage to each part of Rome.

   Upon the bridge called Ponte Angelo   35

   Erected is a castle passing strong,

   Within whose walls such store of ordinance are,

   And double cannons, framed of carved brass,

   As match the days within one complete year;

   Besides the gates, and high pyramides   40

   Which Julius Caesar brought from Africa.

FAUSTUS

   Now by the kingdoms of infernal rule,

   Of Styx, Acheron, and the fiery lake

---

23 *Faustus, I have* From this point the A- and B-texts are only occasionally similar; B's
     version of the remainder of the scene is printed in the Appendix.

24 *privy chamber* a room for personal not public use

27–41 Mephastophilis may have illustrated his little talk with reference to a topographical
     drawing of the city in the form of a stage hanging or painted cut-out, since a 'sittie
     of Rome' is listed in the 1598 Admiral's Men's inventory of properties in the Henslowe
     papers (*Henslowe's Diary*, ed. Foakes and Rickert, 1961, p. 319).

30 *underprop* B (underprops A)

31–2 The lines are supplied in the B-text to supply an obvious deficiency in A (the 'stately
     bridges' must have something to lean over).

35–6 *Upon . . . strong* The Ponte Angelo was built in A.D 135 by Hadrian, whose mausoleum
     (directly facing the bridge but never standing on it) became the Castello di S. Angelo.

37 *ordinance* ordnance, military supplies, artillery

38 *double cannons* cannons of very high calibre

40–1 *pyramides . . . Africa* the obelisk that stands in front of St Peter's; the description
     follows *EFB*, but it was in fact brought from Egypt by the emperor Caligula. The
     plural form *pyramides* is often used for the singular: here the extra syllable is needed
     for the regular pentameter.

43–4 *Styx . . . Phlegethon* the rivers in Hades, the Greek underworld

Of ever-burning Phlegethon, I swear
That I do long to see the monuments   45
And situation of bright-splendent Rome.
Come therefore, let's away.

MEPHASTOPHILIS
Nay Faustus stay, I know you'd fain see the pope,
And take some part of holy Peter's feast,
Where thou shalt see a troup of bald-pate friars,   50
Whose *summum bonum* is in belly-cheer.

FAUSTUS
Well, I am content to compass then some sport,
And by their folly make us merriment.
Then charm me that I may be invisible, to do what I please unseen
of any whilst I stay in Rome.   55

MEPHASTOPHILIS [*casts a spell on him*]
So Faustus, now do what thou wilt, thou shall not be discerned.

Sound a sennet; enter the POPE *and the* CARDINAL OF LORRAINE
to the banquet, with FRIARS *attending*

POPE
My lord of Lorraine, will't please you draw near.

FAUSTUS
Fall to; and the devil choke you and you spare.

POPE
How now, who's that which spake? Friars, look about.

1 FRIAR
Here's nobody, if it like your holiness.   60

POPE
My lord, here is a dainty dish was sent me from the bishop of Milan.

FAUSTUS
I thank you, sir.   *Snatch it*

POPE

46   *situation* lay-out
     bright-splendent resplendent
51   *summum bonum* greatest good; in scholastic theology this is a term used to
     describe the Almighty
52   *compass* contrive, plot, perhaps playing on the rounded bellies of the friars.
58   *Fall to* Get on with it
     and you if you
     spare eat sparingly

51

How now, who's that which snatched the meat from me? Will no
man look? My lord, this dish was sent me from the cardinal of
Florence. 65

FAUSTUS
You say true? I'll have't. [*Snatch it*]

POPE
What, again! My lord, I'll drink to your grace.

FAUSTUS
I'll pledge your grace. [*Snatch the cup*]

LORRAINE
My lord, it may be some ghost newly crept out of purgatory come
to beg a pardon of your holiness. 70

POPE
It may be so; friars, prepare a dirge to lay the fury of this ghost.
Once again my lord, fall to. *The* POPE *crosseth himself*

FAUSTUS
What, are you crossing of your self? Well, use that trick no more,
I would advise you. *Cross again*

FAUSTUS
Well, there's the second time; aware the third! I give you fair warning. 75

Cross again, and FAUSTUS *hits him a box of the ear,*
and they all run away

FAUSTUS
Come on Mephastophilis, what shall we do?

MEPHASTOPHILIS
Nay, I know not; we shall be cursed with bell, book, and candle.

FAUSTUS
How! Bell, book, and candle; candle, book, and bell,

68 *pledge* toast
70 *pardon* papal indulgence
70 *dirge* a corruption of *dirige*, which starts the antiphon at Matins in the Office for the
Dead; hence any requiem mass. The word is used correctly here by the pope, but the
ritual performed is not in fact a mass but a formal cursing.
72 s.d. *crosseth himself EFB* describes how the pope 'would ever be blessing and crossing
over his mouth'. If making the sign of the cross were an effective guard against spirits,
Faustus and Mephastophilis should be overcome by this—hence, comically perhaps,
Faustus's alarm here.
75 *aware* beware
77 *bell, book, and candle* At the close of the Office of Excommunication the bell is tolled,
the bible closed, and the candle extinguished.

Forward and backward, to curse Faustus to hell.
Anon you shall hear a hog grunt, a calf bleat, and an ass bray,   80
Because it is St Peter's holy day.

Enter all the FRIARS *to sing the Dirge*

1 FRIAR
Come brethren, let's about our business with good devotion.
                                                            Sing this
    Cursed be he that stole away his holiness' meat from the table.
        Maledicat Dominus.
    Cursed be he that struck his holiness a blow on the face.   85
        Maledicat Dominus.
    Cursed be he that took Friar Sandelo a blow on the pate.
        Maledicat Dominus.
    Cursed be he that disturbeth our holy dirge.
        Maledicat Dominus.   90
    Cursed be he that took away his holiness' wine.
        Maledicat dominus.
            Et omnes sancti. Amen.
Beat the Friars, and fling fireworks among them, and so Exeunt

79 *forward and backward* compare 3.9
84 *Maledicat Dominus* May the Lord curse him
87 *took* gave
    Sandelo the name probably suggested by the friar's sandals
93 *Et omnes sancti* and all the saints

[Scene 9]

Enter ROBIN [*with conjuring book*] *and* RAFE *with a silver goblet*

ROBIN

Come Rafe, did not I tell thee we were for ever made by this Doctor
Faustus' book? *Ecce signum!* [*Pointing to the goblet*] Here's a simple
purchase for horse-keepers: our horses shall eat no hay as long as
this lasts.

Enter the VINTNER

RAFE

But Robin, here comes the vintner.   5

ROBIN

Hush, I'll gull him supernaturally! Drawer, I hope all is paid; God
be with you. Come, Rafe.   [*They start to go*]

VINTNER

Soft sir, a word with you. I must yet have a goblet paid from you
ere you go.

ROBIN

I a goblet, Rafe! I a goblet? I scorn you: and you are but a &c ...   10
I a goblet? Search me.

VINTNER

I mean so, sir, with your favour.   [*Searches* ROBIN]

Scene 9   In the A-text, this scene runs directly on from the previous Robin and Rafe scene
(Scene 6) even though time has evidently passed; see pp. xxii–xxiii. The B-text version
of this scene is printed in the Appendix.

  1   *for ever made* permanently advantaged, granted success in life

  2   *Ecce signum* behold the proof – a fairly common catchword amongst Elizabethan
comic actors: see *1 Henry IV*, where Falstaff shows his 'sword hack'd like a handsaw
– *ecce signum*' (II.iv.168). Here it satirises what to Protestants was the 'conjuring' of
the Roman Catholic mass in turning wine in the Eucharistic chalice or goblet into
the blood of Christ.
simple purchase clear profit

  3   *eat no hay* i.e. eat well

  5   *vintner* inn-keeper, wine merchant. Rafe has cause to be alarmed since throughout
the scene he is repeatedly made to hold the stolen goblet.

  6   *gull* trick
Drawer one who draws beer. Robin insults the vintner's status.

 10   *but a &c* This gives the actor permission to ad-lib abusively

ROBIN

How say you now?

VINTNER

I must say somewhat to your fellow; you sir!

RAFE

Me sir! Me sir? [ROBIN *takes goblet from him*] Search your fill.   15
[VINTNER *searches* RAFE] Now sir, you may be ashamed to burden
honest men with a matter of truth.

VINTNER

Well, t'one of you hath this goblet about you.

ROBIN

[*Aside*]You lie, drawer, 'tis afore me. [*To the* VINTNER] Sirra you,
I'll teach ye to impeach honest men: [*To* RAFE] stand by; [*To the*   20
VINTNER] I'll scour you for a goblet; stand aside, you had best; I
charge you in the name of Belzebub – look to the goblet, Rafe!

VINTNER

What mean you, sirra?

ROBIN

I'll tell you what I mean: [*He reads*] Sanctobulorum Peri-
phrasticon – nay, I'll tickle you, vintner – look to the goblet,   25
Rafe – Polypragmos Belseborams framanto pacostiphos tostis
Mephastophilis, &c . . .

Enter MEPHASTOPHILIS [*unseen by them*]:
sets squibs at their backs: they run about

VINTNER

O nomine Domine! What mean'st thou Robin, thou hast no goblet?

19   *afore me* (playing on *about you*, l. 18). Robin is holding the goblet in front of him,
        hidden perhaps in a bag or under clothing.
21   *scour* beat, scourge, punish
22, 25   *look . . . goblet* Robin appears to be trying to pass the goblet to Rafe
24–7   a mixture of Latin- and Greek-sounding gibberish; *periphrasis* is a rhetorical term
        for 'roundabout', wordy language; *polypragmon* is Greek for busybody
25   *tickle* beat
28–31   In the panic and chaos caused by the fireworks, the Vintner sees his goblet, Rafe
        gives it to him and Robin pleads to the devil for forgiveness. The Latin phrases recall
        parts of the liturgy but are all corrupt to a greater or lesser extent: *In nomine Domini*
        ('in the name of God'); *Peccatum peccatorum*, 'sin of sins', recalls the structure 'King
        of kings' but also seems to be a misquotation from St Augustine, *peccata pecca-
        torum*, 'of sins upon sins' in Sermon 83 (sometimes number 33) based on Matthew
        xviii, 21–23 concerning Christian redemption; *Misericordia nobis* i.e. *miserere
        nobis*, 'have mercy on us' (*misericordia* is the noun 'pity').

RAFE

Peccatum peccatorum! Here's thy goblet, good Vintner.

ROBIN

Misericordia pro nobis! What shall I do? Good devil, forgive me 30
now, and I'll never rob thy library more.

Enter to them MEPHASTOPHILIS

MEPHASTOPHILIS

Vanish villains, th'one like an ape, an other like a bear, the third
an ass, for doing this enterprise.

[*Exit* VINTNER]

Monarch of hell, under whose black survey
Great potentates do kneel with awful fear; 35
Upon whose altars thousand souls do lie;
How am I vexed with these villains' charms!
From Constantinople am I hither come,
Only for pleasure of these damned slaves.

ROBIN

How, from Constantinople? You have had a great journey! Will 40
you take sixpence in your purse to pay for your supper, and be
gone?

MEPHASTOPHILIS

Well villains, for your presumption, I transform thee into an ape,
and thee into a dog; and so be gone. *Exit*

ROBIN

How, into an ape? That's brave: I'll have fine sport with the boys; 45
I'll get nuts and apples enow.

RAFE

And I must be a dog.

ROBIN

I'faith, thy head will never be out of the potage pot.

Exeunt

---

31 s.d. *Enter to them* This suggests that he is now visible to them, having been invisible
when he brought the fireworks.
32–33 *ape . . . ass* Mephastophilis angrily dismisses Robin and Rafe as ape and bear, and
the Vintner as ass. While the Vintner must be glad to exit, with or without his cup,
Robin, who thinks he has conjured Mephastophilis and has power to dismiss him
(compare 3.40–6), is only scared off a little and comes back with Rafe in tow.
48 *potage* porridge

[Chorus 3]

Enter CHORUS

CHORUS
　　When Faustus had with pleasure ta'en the view
　　Of rarest things, and royal courts of kings,
　　He stayed his course, and so returned home;
　　Where such as bare his absence but with grief –
　　I mean his friends and nearest companions –　　　　　5
　　Did gratulate his safety with kind words.
　　And in their conference of what befell,
　　Touching his journey through the world and air,
　　They put forth questions of astrology,
　　Which Faustus answered with such learned skill,　　　10
　　As they admired and wondered at his wit.
　　Now is his fame spread forth in every land:
　　Amongst the rest the emperor is one,
　　Carolus the fifth, at whose palace now
　　Faustus is feasted 'mongst his noblemen.　　　　　　15
　　What there he did in trial of his art
　　I leave untold: your eyes shall see performed.　　　　　*Exit*

Chorus 3　This Chorus occurs immediately after the Rome scene in the A-text and is missing
　　　　from the B-text where Mephastophilis ends Scene 9 by saying he goes to join Faustus
　　　　at the great Turk's court—an episode which occurs in neither text, although it is a
　　　　feature of the sequel to *EFB*.
　　3　*stayed his course* ceased his journey
　　6　*gratulate* express joy
　11　*As* that
　14　*Carolus* Charles V (1519–56), whose court was at Innsbruck

[Scene 10]

Enter EMPEROR, FAUSTUS, *and a* KNIGHT,
with Attendants [*and* MEPHASTOPHILIS, *invisible*]

EMPEROR

Master Doctor Faustus, I have heard strange report of thy knowledge in the black art, how that none in my empire, nor in the
whole world, can compare with thee for the rare effects of magic.
They say thou hast a familiar spirit, by whom thou canst
accomplish what thou list! This therefore is my request: that thou   5
let me see some proof of thy skill, that mine eyes may be witnesses
to confirm what mine ears have heard reported. And here I swear
to thee, by the honour of mine imperial crown, that whatever thou
dost, thou shalt be no ways prejudiced or endamaged.

KNIGHT *Aside*

I'faith, he looks much like a conjuror.   10

FAUSTUS

My gracious sovereign, though I must confess myself far inferior
to the report men have published, and nothing answerable to the
honour of your imperial majesty, yet for that love and duty binds
me thereunto, I am content to do whatsoever your majesty shall
command me.   15

EMPEROR

Then Doctor Faustus, mark what I shall say. As I was sometime
solitary set within my closet, sundry thoughts arose about the
honour of mine ancestors – how they had won by prowess such
exploits, got such riches, subdued so many kingdoms, as we that
do succeed, or they that shall hereafter possess our throne, shall   20
(I fear me) never attain to that degree of high renown and great
authority. Amongst which kings is Alexander the Great, chief spectacle of the world's pre-eminence:

Scene 10 B's much-expanded version of this scene is printed in the Appendix.
   16 *sometime* recently
   17 *set* sitting
        closet small private room for contemplation, prayer, study etc.
18–22 The extraordinary rise of the Hapsburg family, and their prolonged influence and
        power over most of continental Europe, largely through strategic marriage alliances
        rather than military conquest, is still a source of wonder to historians.

The bright shining of whose glorious acts
Lightens the world with his reflecting beams;   25
As when I hear but motion made of him,
It grieves my soul I never saw the man.
If therefore thou, by cunning of thine art,
Canst raise this man from hollow vaults below,
Where lies entombed this famous conqueror,   30
And bring with him his beauteous paramour,
Both in their right shapes, gesture, and attire
They used to wear during their time of life,
Thou shalt both satisfy my just desire,
And give me cause to praise thee whilst I live.   35

FAUSTUS

My gracious lord, I am ready to accomplish your request, so far
forth as by art and power of my spirit I am able to perform.

KNIGHT *Aside*

I'faith, that's just nothing at all.

FAUSTUS

But, if it like your grace, it is not in my ability to present before
your eyes the true substantial bodies of those two deceased princes   40
which long since are consumed to dust.

KNIGHT *Aside*

Ay, marry, master doctor, now there's a sign of grace in you, when
you will confess the truth.

FAUSTUS

But such spirits as can lively resemble Alexander and his paramour
shall appear before your grace, in that manner that they best   45
lived in, in their most flourishing estate: which I doubt not shall
sufficiently content your imperial majesty.

22 *Alexander the Great* Alexander III of Macedon (356–323 B.C.), pupil of Aristotle,
    conqueror of the Persian Empire, Iran and Northern India, and a subject for numerous
    heroic romances in medieval Europe
26 *motion* mention
31 *paramour* mistress, lover, consort. This is often assumed to be Roxana, a beautiful
    captured Bactrian princess and one of Alexander's many wives. A more elaborate
    dumb-show in the B-text involves Alexander's defeat of the Persian king Darius, in
    which case she might be the whore Thais who at a drunken banquet is sometimes
    supposed to have persuaded Alexander to burn Darius's city of Persepolis (see
    Diodorus Siculus, Bk. 17, Ch. 7 Athenaeus xiii.576, 585). This would link thematically
    with the show of Helen and the burning of Troy (12.90; see Nigel Alexander, 1972,
    pp. 14–19).
42 *marry* a mild oath, 'by the virgin Mary'
44 *lively* 'to the life', vividly

EMPEROR

Go to, master doctor, let me see them presently.

KNIGHT

Do you hear, master doctor? You bring Alexander and his paramour before the emperor! 50

FAUSTUS

How then, sir?

KNIGHT

I'faith, that's as true as Diana turned me to a stag.

FAUSTUS

No sir; but when Actaeon died, he left the horns for you! [*Aside*] Mephastophilis, begone!

Exit MEPHASTOPHILIS [FAUSTUS *starts to conjure*]

KNIGHT

Nay, and you go to conjuring I'll be gone. 55

Exit KNIGHT

FAUSTUS

I'll meet with you anon for interrupting me so. Here they are, my gracious lord.

Enter MEPHASTOPHILIS
with ALEXANDER *and his* PARAMOUR

EMPEROR

Master doctor, I heard this lady, while she lived, had a wart or mole in her neck; how shall I know whether it be so or no?

FAUSTUS

Your highness may boldly go and see. 60

Exit ALEXANDER [*and his* PARAMOUR]

48   *Go to* a mild rebuke, 'enough', 'get on with it'
     presently immediately
53   *Actaeon* As a punishment for coming upon the goddess Diana and her nymphs
     when they were bathing, Actaeon was turned into a stag, and his own hounds tore
     him to pieces.
56   *meet with you* a) meet you, b) be even with you
60   s.d. *Exit Alexander* A. Editors usually add a s.d. here instructing the Emperor to
     inspect the neck of Alexander's paramour as happens in the B-text, delaying
     Alexander's exit until after the Emperor's next speech. It is, however, rather more
     in Alexander's character, and his status as conqueror of such a vast Empire, if he
     prevents this Emperor's presumption, exiting immediately, as marked in the A-
     text. This would also prompt the Emperor's admiration at l. 61 and his conviction
     that these apparitions are genuine—as there can be few, if any, people in his
     experience who would be so bold as to deny him.

EMPEROR

Sure, these are no spirits, but the true substantial bodies of those
two deceased princes.

FAUSTUS

Will't please your highness now to send for the knight that was
so pleasant with me here of late?

EMPEROR

One of you call him forth.   65

Enter the KNIGHT *with a pair of horns on his head*

How now sir knight? Why, I had thought thou hadst been a
bachelor, but now I see thou hast a wife that not only gives thee
horns but makes thee wear them! Feel on thy head.

KNIGHT

Thou damned wretch and execrable dog,
Bred in the concave of some monstrous rock,   70
How dar'st thou thus abuse a gentleman?
Villain I say, undo what thou hast done.

FAUSTUS

O not so fast sir, there's no haste but good. Are you remembered
how you crossed me in my conference with the emperor? I think
I have met with you for it.   75

EMPEROR

Good master doctor, at my entreaty release him; he hath done
penance sufficient.

FAUSTUS

My gracious lord, not so much for the injury he offered me here
in your presence, as to delight you with some mirth, hath Faustus
worthily requited this injurious knight; which being all I desire, 80
I am content to release him of his horns. And, sir knight, hereafter
speak well of scholars: [*Aside*] Mephastophilis, transform him

---

64 *pleasant* facetious, jesting
67 *bachelor* a) i.e. knight bachelor, a member of the lowest order of knighthood, b)
      unmarried man
67–8 *wife ... wear them* It was an old joke that the cuckolded husband would grow horns
      to publish his shame.
70 *Bred ... rock. See Tamburlaine*, III.ii.89: 'Fenc'd with the concave of some monstrous
      rock'.
73 *Are you remembered* Have you forgotten
75 *met with you* am even with you
78 *injury* insult

straight. [*To* EMPEROR] Now my good lord, having done my duty,
I humbly take my leave.

EMPEROR

Farewell master doctor, yet ere you go, expect from me a bounteous 85
reward.

Exit EMPEROR [*and his Attendants*]

FAUSTUS

Now Mephastophilis, the restless course
That time doth run with calm and silent foot,
Shortening my days and thread of vital life,
Calls for the payment of my latest years; 90
Therefore, sweet Mephastophilis, let us make haste to Wittenberg.

MEPHASTOPHILIS

What, will you go on horseback, or on foot?

FAUSTUS

Nay, till I am past this fair and pleasant green, I'll walk on foot.

Enter a HORSE-COURSER

HORSE-COURSER

I have been all this day seeking one Master Fustian: 'mass, see where
he is! God save you, master doctor. 95

FAUSTUS

What, horse-courser: you are well met.

HORSE-COURSER

Do you hear, sir; I have brought you forty dollars for your horse.

87–93   Faustus and Mephastophilis walk back to Wittenberg, meeting the Horse-courser
on the way. Lines 87–93 occur only in the A-text. A different version of lines 94–163
occurs in the B-text as a separate scene. This is printed in the Appendix as Scene 10c,
and follows an extra scene (10b) in which Benvolio tries to get his revenge on Faustus.

89   *thread of vital life* The image of life as a single thread comes from Greek mythology.

90   *payment* The idea of death as a debt owed to nature is a commonplace (See *Macbeth*,
V.ix.5: 'Your son, my lord, has paid a soldier's debt'); but it is revitalized here by
Faustus' predicament.
   latest last

93   s.d HORSE-COURSER Horse-dealer; a reputation for dishonesty has always attached
to such traders

94   *Fustian* The Horse-courser, in mispronouncing Faustus's name, using a word for the
kind of coarse cloth he himself would wear, unwittingly puns on 'bombastic or made-
up language'; compare the clown's use of the word at 4.70, which may suggest that
one actor played both parts.

97   *dollars* English name for certain foreign coins including the German silver thaler,
later in the scene punning on 'dolours', physical or mental suffering

FAUSTUS

I cannot sell him so: if thou lik'st him for fifty, take him.

HOURSE-COURSER

Alas sir, I have no more. [*To* MEPHASTOPHILIS] I pray you speak
for me.   100

MEPHASTOPHILIS

I pray you let him have him; he is an honest fellow, and he has a
great charge – neither wife nor child.

FAUSTUS

Well; come, give me your money; my boy will deliver him to you.
But I must tell you one thing before you have him: ride him not
into the water at any hand.   105

HORSE-COURSER

Why sir, will he not drink of all waters?

FAUSTUS

O yes, he will drink of all waters, but ride him not into the water.
Ride him over hedge or ditch, or where thou wilt, but not into the
water.

HORSE-COURSER

Well sir. Now am I made man for ever: I'll not leave my horse for   110
forty! If he had but the quality of hey ding ding, hey ding ding,
I'd make a brave living on him! He has a buttock as slick as an eel.
Well, God b'y sir; your boy will deliver him me? But hark ye sir,
if my horse be sick, or ill at ease, if I bring his water to you, you'll
tell me what it is?   115

FAUSTUS

Away, you villain! What, dost think I am a horse-doctor?

                                                              Exit HORSE-COURSER

102 *charge* expenses
      wife nor child playing on the proverb 'wife and children are bills of charge'
103 *boy* servant, in this case Mephastophilis
105 *at any hand* whatever happens
106 *drink of all waters* go anywhere
110 *made man* well set up
      leave part with
111 *forty* a common term for 'any large amount', but of course forty is exactly what he
      paid
      quality of hey ding ding The Horse-courser seems to be wishing that the horse were
      a stallion, not a gelding; compare Nashe, *Have With You to Saffron Walden* (1596):
      'Yea, Madam *Gabriele*, are you such an old ierker? then Hey ding a ding, vp with
      your perticoate, haue at your plum-tree' (McKerrow iii, p. 113).
114 *his water* his urine (for diagnosis)
116 s.d. *Exit* HORSE-COURSER This s.d. occurs after the previous line in the A-text for
      reasons of space.

What art thou, Faustus, but a man condemned to die?
Thy fatal time doth draw to final end.
Despair doth drive distrust unto my thoughts;
Confound these passions with a quiet sleep. 120
Tush, Christ did call the thief upon the cross;
Then rest thee, Faustus, quiet in conceit.

Sleep in his chair

Enter HORSE-COURSER *all wet, crying*

HORSE-COURSER
Alas, alas, Doctor Fustian, quoth 'a: 'mass, Doctor Lopus was never
such a doctor! H'as given me a purgation, h'as purged me of forty
dollars! I shall never see them more. But yet, like an ass as I was, 125
I would not be ruled by him; for he bade me I should ride him
into no water. Now I, thinking my horse had had some rare quality
that he would not have had me known of, I, like a vent'rous youth,
rid him into the deep pond at the town's end. I was no sooner in
the middle of the pond, but my horse vanished away, and I sat 130
upon a bottle of hay, never so near drowning in my life! But I'll
seek out my doctor, and have my forty dollars again, or I'll make
it the dearest horse. O, yonder is his snipper-snapper! Do you hear,
you hey-pass, where's your master?

MEPHASTOPHILIS
Why sir, what would you? You cannot speak with him. 135

HORSE-COURSER
But I will speak with him.

MEPHASTOPHILIS
Why, he's fast asleep; come some other time.

118 *fatal time* time of death, allotted by fate
121 *Christ . . . cross* St Luke's Gospel tells of Christ's words of comfort to the crucified
     thief: 'This day shalt thou be with me in paradise' (xxiii, 43)
122 *in conceit* in this thought
     s.d. *in his chair* Presumably at some point during the previous speech he has opened
     a curtain at the back of the stage to reveal his study in Wittenberg (see line 91).
123 *Doctor Lopus* This joke must have found its way into the text after the execution, in
     February 1594, of Roderigo Lopez, Queen Elizabeth's personal physician, who was
     accused of plotting to poison her.
124–5 *purgation . . . dollars* with reference to the proverb 'give one's purse a purgation'
128 *known of* aware of
131 *bottle* bundle
134 *hey-pass* a conjuror's 'magic' catchphrase

HORSE-COURSER
  I'll speak with him now, or I'll break his glass-windows about his
  ears.
MEPHASTOPHILIS
  I tell thee, he has not slept this eight nights.   140
HORSE-COURSER
  And he have not slept this eight weeks I'll speak with him.
MEPHASTOPHILIS
  See where he is, fast asleep.
HORSE-COURSER
  Ay, this is he; God save ye master doctor, master doctor, master
  Doctor Fustian, forty dollars, forty dollars for a bottle of hay.
MEPHASTOPHILIS
  Why, thou seest he hears thee not.   145
HORSE-COURSER
  So ho ho; so ho ho.   *Halloo in his ear*
  No, will you not wake? I'll make you wake ere I go.
                          Pull him by the leg, and pull it away
  Alas, I am undone! What shall I do?
FAUSTUS
  O my leg, my leg! Help, Mephastophilis! Call the officers! My leg,
  my leg!   150
MEPHASTOPHILIS
  Come villain, to the constable.
HORSE-COURSER
  O Lord, sir! Let me go, and I'll give you forty dollars more.
MEPHASTOPHILIS
  Where be they?
HORSE-COURSER
  I have none about me: come to my ostry and I'll give them you.
MEPHASTOPHILIS
  Begone quickly!   155
                                            HORSE-COURSER *runs away*
FAUSTUS
  What, is he gone? Farewell he: Faustus has his leg again, and the
  horse-courser – I take it – a bottle of hay for his labour! Well, this
  trick shall cost him forty dollars more.

138 *glass-windows* spectacles
146 *So ho ho* the huntsman's cry when he catches sight of the quarry
154 *ostry* hostelry, inn

Enter WAGNER

How now Wagner, what's the news with thee?

WAGNER

Sir, the Duke of Vanholt doth earnestly entreat your company. 160

FAUSTUS

The Duke of Vanholt! An honourable gentleman, to whom I must be no niggard of my cunning. Come Mephastophilis, let's away to him.

Exeunt

160   Vanholt i.e. Anhalt (as in the source) a Duchy in central Germany

[Scene 11]

[Enter FAUSTUS *with* MEPHASTOPHILIS, *invisible]*
Enter to them the DUKE *and the* DUCHESS; *the* DUKE *speaks*

DUKE

Believe me, master doctor, this merriment hath much pleased me.

FAUSTUS

My gracious Lord, I am glad it contents you so well: but it may
be, madam, you take no delight in this; I have heard that great-
bellied women do long for some dainties or other – what is it,
madam? Tell me, and you shall have it.   5

DUCHESS

Thanks, good master doctor; and for I see your courteous intent
to pleasure me, I will not hide from you the thing my heart desires.
And were it now summer, as it is January and the dead time of
the winter, I would desire no better meat than a dish of ripe grapes.

FAUSTUS

Alas madam, that's nothing! *[Aside]* Mephastophilis, begone!   10
      Exit MEPHASTOPHILIS
Were it a greater thing than this, so it would content you, you
should have it.

Enter MEPHASTOPHILIS *with the grapes*

Here they be, madam; will't please you taste on them?

DUKE

Believe me, master doctor, this makes me wonder above the rest:
that being in the dead time of winter, and in the month of January,   15
how you should come by these grapes.

0.2 s.d. *Enter to them . . . speaks* The A-text's slightly unusual stage direction suggests
   that Faustus and Mephastophilis have either remained on stage from the previous
   scene, or re-entered before the Duke and Duchess. Either there is then some unscripted
   business with sound effects (see *this merriment* l. 1), indicating the staging of a magic
   show off stage, or perhaps an additional scene took place which was written on a
   separate leaf of the manuscript and has not survived. The B-text has a tavern scene
   in which a Carter recounts a story about Faustus swindling him out of a load of hay,
   and the Horse-courser responds by retelling the story we have just witnessed; these
   characters are then conjured back at the end of the scene for the further entertainment
   of the Duke and Duchess.
3–4 *great-bellied* pregnant
 9 *meat* food

67

FAUSTUS

If it like your grace, the year is divided into two circles over the whole world, that when it is here winter with us, in the contrary circle it is summer with them, as in India, Saba, and farther countries in the east; and by means of a swift spirit that I have, I had   20 them brought hither, as ye see. How do you like them, madam; be they good?

DUCHESS

Believe me, master doctor, they be the best grapes that e'er I tasted in my life before.

FAUSTUS

I am glad they content you so, madam.   25

DUKE

Come madam, let us in, where you must well reward this learned man for the great kindness he hath showed to you.

DUCHESS

And so I will my lord; and whilst I live, rest beholding for this courtesy.

FAUSTUS

I humbly thank your grace.   30

DUKE

Come, master doctor, follow us, and receive your reward.

                         Exeunt

17   *two circles* The explanation is confusing. The relevant circles would be the northern and southern hemispheres, but the author appears to be thinking in terms of east and west; *EFB* evades the matter while providing the detail of the twice-yearly fruit.
19   *Saba* Sheba; in modern times, this is the Yemen
28   *rest beholding* remain indebted

[Scene 12]

Enter WAGNER *solus*

WAGNER

    I think my master means to die shortly,
    For he hath given to me all his goods!
    And yet methinks, if that death were near,
    He would not banquet, and carouse, and swill
    Amongst the students, as even now he doth,   5
    Who are at supper with such belly-cheer,
    As Wagner ne'er beheld in all his life.
    See where they come: belike the feast is ended.   [*Exit*]

Enter FAUSTUS [*and* MEPHASTOPHILIS],
with two or three SCHOLARS

1 SCHOLAR

    Master Doctor Faustus, since our conference about fair ladies,
    which was the beautifullest in all the world, we have determined   10
    with ourselves that Helen of Greece was the admirablest lady
    that ever lived. Therefore, master doctor, if you will do us that
    favour as to let us see that peerless dame of Greece, whom all the
    world admires for majesty, we should think ourselves much
    beholding unto you.   15

FAUSTUS

    Gentlemen for that I know your friendship is unfeigned,
    And Faustus' custom is not to deny
    The just requests of those that wish him well,
    You shall behold that peerless dame of Greece,
    No otherways for pomp and majesty   20

Scene 12 The A- and B-text versions of this scene are closely related; but see Intro. pp. xxvii–xviii.

  0.1 s.d. *Enter* WAGNER *solus* Again, Wagner performs the function of Chorus, but this time in his role as Faustus's servant.

    6 *belly-cheer* food and drink

 10–11 *beautifullest . . . admirablest* The clumsy form of these superlatives will help an actor to appear drunk on too much *belly-cheer*.

   11 *Helen of Greece* The wife of Menelaus, king of Sparta, who was given to the Trojan prince Paris as a reward for judging which of the three goddesses Hera, Athena and Aphrodite was the most beautiful. Thus began the ten-year Trojan war.

 16–23 as prose in A

Than when Sir Paris crossed the seas with her,
And brought the spoils to rich Dardania.
Be silent then, for danger is in words

Music sounds, and HELEN *passeth over the stage*

2 SCHOLAR

Too simple is my wit to tell her praise,
Whom all the world admires for majesty.   25

3 SCHOLAR

No marvel though the angry Greeks pursued
With ten years' war the rape of such a queen,
Whose heavenly beauty passeth all compare.

1 SCHOLAR

Since we have seen the pride of Nature's works,
And only paragon of excellence,   30

Enter an OLD MAN

Let us depart; and for this glorious deed
Happy and blest be Faustus evermore.

FAUSTUS

Gentlemen farewell; the same I wish to you.

                                        Exeunt SCHOLARS

OLD MAN

Ah Doctor Faustus, that I might prevail
To guide thy steps unto the way of life –   35
By which sweet path thou may'st attain the goal –
That shall conduct thee to celestial rest.
Break heart, drop blood, and mingle it with tears,
Tears falling from repentant heaviness

21 *Sir* The title was often applied to classical heroes in medieval romance.
22 *Dardania* Troy; in fact the city built by Dardanus on the Hellespont, but the name
    is often transferred to Troy
23 s.d. *passeth over* crosses
26 *pursued* followed up; with the sense of attacked, besieged (*OED* 6b)
27 *rape* a) abduction, b) rape
30 *paragon of excellence* Helen was not herself accounted blameless in most versions of
    the story.
36–7 *By . . . rest* Either the Old Man repeats himself in his anxiety (or perhaps as a
    characterisation of old age), or the manuscript contained alternative lines, marked
    in this edition by dashes.

Of thy most vile and loathsome filthiness,   40
The stench whereof corrupts the inward soul
With such flagitious crimes of heinous sins,
As no commiseration may expel;
But mercy, Faustus, of thy saviour sweet,
Whose blood alone must wash away thy guilt.   45

FAUSTUS
Where art thou Faustus? Wretch, what hast thou done!
Damned art thou Faustus, damned; despair and die!
Hell calls for right, and with a roaring voice
Says, 'Faustus, come: thine hour is come'!

          MEPHASTOPHILIS *gives him a dagger*
And Faustus will come to do thee right.   50

OLD MAN
Ah stay, good Faustus, stay thy desperate steps!
I see an angel hovers o'er thy head,
And with a vial full of precious grace
Offers to pour the same into thy soul!
Then call for mercy, and avoid despair.   55

FAUSTUS
Ah my sweet friend, I feel thy words
To comfort my distressed soul;
Leave me awhile to ponder on my sins.

OLD MAN
I go, sweet Faustus; but with heavy cheer,
Fearing the ruin of thy hopeless soul.   [*Exit*]   60

FAUSTUS
Accursed Faustus, where is mercy now?
I do repent, and yet I do despair:
Hell strives with grace for conquest in my breast!
What shall I do to shun the snares of death?

MEPHASTOPHILIS
Thou traitor, Faustus: I arrest thy soul   65

---

42 *flagitious* extremely wicked
43 *commiseration* pity, compassion, perhaps 'miseration' (obs.) mercy
49 s.d. MEPHASTOPHILIS ... *dagger* The s.d. is inserted in the margin at this point in the
    A-text. In this position, the appearance of the dagger is a terrible (and perhaps ironic)
    response to Faustus's sin of despair. Some editors, however, insert the s.d. after line
    47, as in the B-text, where it has the effect merely of prompting the words 'Hell calls'.
50 *do thee right* i.e. pay what is due
59 *heavy cheer* sorrowful frame of mind

For disobedience to my sovereign lord.
Revolt, or I'll in piecemeal tear thy flesh.

FAUSTUS

Sweet Mephastophilis, entreat thy lord
To pardon my unjust presumption;
And with my blood again I will confirm   70
My former vow I made to Lucifer.

MEPHASTOPHILIS

Do it then quickly, with unfeigned heart,
Lest greater danger do attend thy drift.

FAUSTUS

Torment, sweet friend, that base and crooked age
That durst dissuade me from thy Lucifer,   75
With greatest torments that our hell affords.

MEPHASTOPHILIS

His faith is great, I cannot touch his soul,
But what I may afflict his body with,
I will attempt – which is but little worth.

FAUSTUS

One thing, good servant, let me crave of thee,   80
To glut the longing of my heart's desire:
That I might have unto my paramour
That heavenly Helen which I saw of late,
Whose sweet embracings may extinguish clean
These thoughts that do dissuade me from my vow: 85
And keep mine oath I made to Lucifer.

MEPHASTOPHILIS

Faustus, this, or what else thou shalt desire,
Shall be performed in twinkling of an eye.

Enter HELEN

FAUSTUS

Was this the face that launched a thousand ships,
And burnt the topless towers of Ilium?   90

67 *Revolt* Turn again to your allegiance
73 *drift* drifting; also purpose
74 *base . . . age* i.e. the Old Man
84 *clean* completely
89 *Was . . . ships* Compare Lucian's *Dialogues of the Dead*, no.18, where Hermes shows
    Helen's skull to Menippus who responds 'And for this a thousand ships carried
    warriors from every part of Greece' (*The Works of Lucian*, vol.1, 1935, pp. 137–8).

Sweet Helen, make me immortal with a kiss:
Her lips sucks forth my soul, see where it flies!
Come Helen, come, give me my soul again.
Here will I dwell, for heaven be in these lips,
And all is dross that is not Helena!   95

Enter OLD MAN

I will be Paris, and for love of thee,
Instead of Troy shall Wittenberg be sacked;
And I will combat with weak Menelaus,
And wear thy colours on my plumed crest:
Yea, I will wound Achilles in the heel,   100
And then return to Helen for a kiss.
O thou art fairer than the evening air,
Clad in the beauty of a thousand stars,
Brighter art thou than flaming Jupiter
When he appeared to hapless Semele;   105
More lovely than the monarch of the sky
In wanton Arethusa's azured arms;
And none but thou shalt be my paramour.
                    Exeunt [FAUSTUS *and* HELEN]

OLD MAN
Accursed Faustus, miserable man,

89–100   In these lines Marlowe is repeating his own memorable phrases:
                Helen, whose beauty summoned Greece to arms,
                And drew a thousand ships to Tenedos.
                                        2 Tamburlaine, II, iv, 87–8
                And he'll make me immortal with a kiss.
                                        Dido, IV, iv, 123
                So thou wouldst prove as true as Paris did,
                Would, as fair Troy was, Carthage might be sacked,
                And I be called a second Helena.
                                        Dido, V,1, 146–8 82
     90   *Ilium* Troy
     95   s.d. The Old Man's entrance here and final speech (109–17) are omitted in the B-text.
     98   *weak* i.e. cuckolded
    100   *wound . . . heel* Achilles was invulnerable apart from one of his heels – where he was
          shot by Paris.
  104–5   *flaming . . . Semele* Jupiter's mortal lover Semele demanded that he come to her in
          his real form. He appeared as a shower of flaming gold, which consumed her.
  106–7   *monarch . . . arms* Arethusa was a nymph who was changed into a fountain after
          bathing in the river Alpheus and exciting the river-god's passion; Alpheus is said to
          have been related to the sun.

That from thy soul exclud'st the grace of heaven, 110
And fliest the throne of His tribunal seat!

Enter the DEVILS

Satan begins to sift me with his pride,
As in this furnace God shall try my faith.
My faith, vile hell, shall triumph over thee!
Ambitious fiends, see how the heavens smiles 115
At your repulse, and laughs your state to scorn.
Hence hell, for hence I fly unto my God.

Exeunt [*by different doors*]

112   *sift* Compare St Luke's Gospel xxii, 3: 'Satan hath desired to have you, that he may
sift you as wheat.'
115   *the heavens* the celestial beings who inhabit the extra-terrestial spheres of the geocentric
universe.
smiles A singular verb following a plural subject is not uncommon in sixteenth-
century literature.

[Scene 13]

Enter FAUSTUS *with the* SCHOLARS

FAUSTUS
Ah gentlemen!

1 SCHOLAR
What ails Faustus?

FAUSTUS
Ah my sweet chamber-fellow, had I lived with thee, then had I
lived still; but now I die eternally. Look, comes he not, comes he
not?   5

2 SCHOLAR
What means Faustus?

3 SCHOLAR
Belike he is grown into some sickness, by being over-solitary.

1 SCHOLAR
If it be so, we'll have physicians to cure him; 'tis but a surfeit, never
fear, man.

FAUSTUS
A surfeit of deadly sin that hath damned both body and soul.   10

2 SCHOLAR
Yet Faustus, look up to heaven; remember God's mercies are
infinite.

FAUSTUS
But Faustus' offence can ne'er be pardoned! The serpent that
tempted Eve may be saved, but not Faustus. Ah gentlemen, hear
me with patience, and tremble not at my speeches, though my   15
heart pants and quivers to remember that I have been a student
here these thirty years – O would I had never seen Wittenberg,
never read book – and what wonders I have done, all Germany
can witness – yea, all the world, for which Faustus hath lost both
Germany and the world, yea, heaven itself – heaven, the seat of   20
God, the throne of the blessed, the kingdom of joy – and must
remain in hell for ever – hell, ah, hell for ever! Sweet friends, what
shall become of Faustus, being in hell for ever?

Scene 13 B opens this scene with the arrival of the devils – Lucifer, Belzebub, and Mephastophilis – who have come to witness Faustus's end; see Appendix 13.1–25.
  16 *pants* races, throbs

75

3 SCHOLAR

Yet Faustus, call on God.

FAUSTUS

On God, whom Faustus hath abjured? On God, whom Faustus   25
hath blasphemed? Ah my God, I would weep, but the devil draws
in my tears! gush forth blood instead of tears – yea, life and soul!
O, he stays my tongue! I would lift up my hands, but see, they hold
them, they hold them!

ALL

Who, Faustus?   30

FAUSTUS

Lucifer and Mephastophilis! Ah gentlemen, I gave them my soul
for my cunning.

ALL

God forbid!

FAUSTUS

God forbade it indeed, but Faustus hath done it: for vain pleasure
of four-and-twenty years hath Faustus lost eternal joy and felicity!   35
I writ them a bill with mine own blood, the date is expired, the
time will come, and he will fetch me.

1 SCHOLAR

Why did not Faustus tell us of this before, that divines might have
prayed for thee?

FAUSTUS

Oft have I thought to have done so, but the devil threatened to   40
tear me in pieces if I named God, to fetch both body and soul, if
I once gave ear to divinity; and now 'tis too late! Gentlemen away,
lest you perish with me.

2 SCHOLAR

O what shall we do to save Faustus?

FAUSTUS

Talk not of me but save yourselves and depart.   45

26–7 *draws in my tears* 'No not so much as their eyes are able to shed tears (thretten and
torture them as ye please) while first they repent (God not permitting them to
dissemble their obstinacie in so horrible a crime)', *Daemonologie*, by James VI and
I (Edinburgh, 1597), p. 81.

28 *stays* holds back

34 *for vain* A (for the vain B)
vain worthless, fruitless

36 *bill* written document, here legal deed or contract

44 *to save Faustus* B (to Faustus A)

3 SCHOLAR

God will strengthen me. I will stay with Faustus.

1 SCHOLAR

Tempt not God, sweet friend, but let us into the next room, and there pray for him.

FAUSTUS

Ay, pray for me, pray for me; and what noise soever ye hear, come not unto me, for nothing can rescue me.   50

2 SCHOLAR

Pray thou, and we will pray that God may have mercy upon thee.

FAUSTUS

Gentlemen, farewell. If I live till morning, I'll visit you; if not, Faustus is gone to hell.

ALL

Faustus, farewell.   *Exeunt* SCHOLARS

The clock strikes eleven

FAUSTUS

Ah Faustus,   55
Now hast thou but one bare hour to live,
And then thou must be damned perpetually.
Stand still, you ever-moving spheres of heaven,
That time may cease, and midnight never come.
Fair Nature's eye, rise, rise again, and make   60
Perpetual day, or let this hour be but
A year, a month, a week, a natural day,
That Faustus may repent and save his soul.
O lente, lente currite noctis equi!
The stars move still, time runs, the clock will strike,   65
The devil will come, and Faustus must be damned.

52   *farewell* See Appendix 13.93–126 for the B-text's insertion at this point.
58-63   Cf. *Edward II*, V.i.64–8:
           Continue ever, thou celestial sun;
           Let never silent night possess this clime:
           Stand still, you watches of the element;
           All times and seasons, rest you at a stay,
           That Edward may be still fair England's king.
60   *Fair Nature's eye* the sun
64   'Go slowly, slowly, you horses of the night': the play's final irony; the line is from Ovid's *Amores*, I, xiii, 40, where the poet longs for never-ending night in his mistress' arms

77

O I'll leap up to my God! Who pulls me down?
See, see where Christ's blood streams in the firmament!
One drop would save my soul, half a drop. ah my Christ –
Ah, rend not my heart for naming of my Christ;   70
Yet will I call on him – O spare me, Lucifer!
Where is it now? 'Tis gone: and see where God
Stretcheth out his arm, and bends his ireful brows!
Mountains and hills, come, come and fall on me,
And hide me from the heavy wrath of God.   75
No, no?
Then will I headlong run into the earth:
Earth, gape! O no, it will not harbour me.
You stars that reigned at my nativity,
Whose influence hath allotted death and hell,   80
Now draw up Faustus like a foggy mist
Into the entrails of yon labouring cloud,
That when you vomit forth into the air
My limbs may issue from your smoky mouths,
So that my soul may but ascend to heaven.   85

The watch strikes

Ah, half the hour is past: 'twill all be past anon.
O God, if thou wilt not have mercy on my soul,
Yet for Christ's sake, whose blood hath ransomed me,
Impose some end to my incessant pain:

67 *leap up* This common Renaissance image is also shown in the woodblock print on
    the title page of the 1604 edition, but the icon's meaning is ambivalent and Faustus's
    aspirations were also the cause of his tragedy; see the reference to Icarus at Chorus
    1.20–2.
72 *it* the vision of Christ's blood; the momentary yielding to terror and the devil banishes
    even this hope of salvation
74–5 'And they shall say to the mountains: Cover us; and to the hills, Fall on us', Hosea
    x, 8 (see also Revelations vi, 16; and St Luke xxiii, 3). The Usurer in *A Looking Glass
    for London* has the same idea:
        Hell gapes for me, heaven will not hold my soule,
        You mountaines shroude me from the God of truth . . .
        Cover me hills, and shroude me from the Lord.
                                                            ll. 2054–5, 9
79–85 *You . . . heaven* Faustus prays the stars, whose positions at his birth ordained this fate,
    to suck him up into a cloud, as a fog or mist is drawn up, and then in a storm expel
    his body in order that his soul may be saved. See Introduction, p. xvii.

Let Faustus live in hell a thousand years,   90
A hundred thousand, and at last be saved.
O, no end is limited to damned souls!
Why wert thou not a creature wanting soul?
Or why is this immortal that thou hast?
Ah, Pythagoras' *metempsychosis* – were that true,   95
This soul should fly from me, and I be changed
Unto some brutish beast:
All beasts are happy, for when they die,
Their souls are soon dissolved in elements;
But mine must live still to be plagued in hell.   100
Cursed be the parents that engendered me:
No Faustus, curse thy self, curse Lucifer,
That hath deprived thee of the joys of heaven!

The clock striketh twelve

O it strikes, it strikes! Now body, turn to air,
Or Lucifer will bear thee quick to hell.   105

Thunder and lightning

O soul, be changed into little water drops,
And fall into the ocean, ne'er be found.
My God, my God, look not so fierce on me!

Enter DEVILS

Adders and serpents, let me breathe awhile!
Ugly hell gape not! Come not, Lucifer!   110
I'll burn my books – ah, Mephastophilis!

                                      Exeunt with him

---

95 *Pythagoras' metempsychosis* the theory of the transmigration of souls, attributed to
Pythagoras, whereby the human soul at the death of the body took on some other form
of life

105 *quick* living

111 *burn my books* All magicians who renounced their art made a solemn act of disposing
of their magic books; cf. *The Tempest*, V.i.56–7: 'deeper than did ever plummet sound
I'll drown my book'.
s.d. *Exeunt with him* The B-text adds a macabre scene where the Scholars discover
Faustus' mangled body (see Appendix 13b).

Enter CHORUS

Cut is the branch that might have grown full straight,
And burned is Apollo's laurel bough,
That sometime grew within this learned man.
Faustus is gone! Regard his hellish fall,   115
Whose fiendful fortune may exhort the wise
Only to wonder at unlawful things:
Whose deepness doth entice such forward wits,
To practise more than heavenly power permits.   [*Exit*]

Terminat hora diem, terminat author opus.

---

113   *Apollo's laurel bough* the wreath of the poet (in this case, conjuror – see scene 3, line 33)
         laureate
         Terminat . . . opus The hour ends the day, the author ends his works. The origin is
         unknown, and it seems likely that the motto, with the final emblem, was appended by
         the printer and not by Marlowe.
         The Latin motto is followed by another printer's device – McKerrow 313: 'Framed device
         of Justice striking a bushel of corn; with SUCH AS I MAKE. SUCH WILL I TAKE'

The title page to the second edition of *Dr Faustus*, the B-text. First published in 1616, this version was reprinted in 1619, 1620, 1624, 1628 and 1631. An inventory of properties belonging to the Admiral's Men who first performed the play at the Rose Theatre in London records that they possessed a dragon for use in this play (see p. xix). The dragon/devil in this picture looks as if it might be appearing through a hole in the floor – or a trapdoor in a stage.

The Tragicall History
of the Life and Death
of Doctor FAVSTVS.

With new additions.

Written by *Ch. Marlo[e],*

Printed at London for *John Wright*, and are to be fold at his
fhop without Newgate. 1628.

APPENDIX

Scenes from the B-text: sometimes these are straightforward additions to the play presented in the A-text; in other cases, the A scenes have been substantially re-worked. The scenes in the Appendix are identified by the numbers of the A-text scenes which they replace or augment.

[Scene 4]

Enter WAGNER *and the* CLOWN

WAGNER
Come hither, sirra boy.

CLOWN
Boy? O disgrace to my person: zounds, boy in your face, you have seen many boys with beards, I am sure.

WAGNER
Sirra, hast thou no comings in?

CLOWN
Yes, and goings out too, you may see sir. 5

WAGNER
Alas poor slave, see how poverty jests in his nakedness. I know the villain's out of service, and so hungry, that I know he would give his soul to the devil, for a shoulder of mutton, tho' it were blood raw.

CLOWN
Not so neither! I had need to have it well roasted, and good sauce 10 to it, if I pay so dear, I can tell you.

WAGNER
Sirra, wilt thou be my man and wait on me? And I will make thee go like *Qui mihi discipulus.*

CLOWN
What, in verse?

WAGNER
No slave, in beaten silk and stavesacre. 15

CLOWN
Stavesacre? That's good to kill vermin: then belike if I serve you, I shall be lousy.

WAGNER
Why, so thou shalt be, whether thou dost it or no: for sirra, if thou dost not presently bind thy self to me for seven years, I'll turn all

the lice about thee into familiars, and make them tear thee in   20
pieces.

CLOWN

Nay sir, you may save yourself a labour, for they are as familiar
with me, as if they paid for their meat and drink, I can tell you.

WAGNER

Well sirra, leave your jesting, and take these guilders.

CLOWN

Yes, marry sir; and I thank you too.   25

WAGNER

So; now thou art to be at an hour's warning, whensoever, and
wheresoever the devil shall fetch thee.

CLOWN

Here, take your guilders; I'll none of 'em.

WAGNER

Not I; thou art pressed! Prepare thyself, for I will presently raise
up two devils to carry thee away: Banio, Belcher!   30

CLOWN

Belcher? and Belcher come here, I'll belch him: I am not afraid of
a devil.

Enter TWO DEVILS

WAGNER

How now, sir; will you serve me now?

CLOWN

Ay, good Wagner; take away the devil, then.

WAGNER

Spirits, away! Now sirra, follow me.   35

CLOWN

I will, sir! But hark you, master – will you teach me this conjuring
occupation?

WAGNER

Ay sirra, I'll teach thee to turn thyself to a dog, or a cat, or a mouse,
or a rat, or anything.

CLOWN

A dog, or a cat, or a mouse, or a rat? O brave, Wagner!   40

WAGNER

Villain, call me Master Wagner; and see that you walk attentively,
and let your right eye be always diametrally fixed upon my left
heel, that thou may'st, 'Quasi vestigias nostras insistere'.

CLOWN

Well sir, I warrant you.

Exeunt

[Scene 6]

Enter the CLOWN [ROBIN]

ROBIN

What, Dick, look to the horses there till I come again. I have gotten one of Doctor Faustus' conjuring books, and now we'll have such knavery as 't passes.

Enter DICK

DICK

What, Robin, you must come away and walk the horses.

ROBIN

I walk the horses! I scorn 't, i'faith. I have other matters in hand.   5
Let the horses walk themselves and they will. [*Reads*] 'A *per se* a,
t. h. e. the; o *per se* o; deny orgon, gorgon'. Keep further from me,
O thou illiterate and unlearned ostler.

DICK

'Snails, what hast thou got there? A book! Why, thou canst not tell
ne'er a word on't.   10

ROBIN

That thou shalt see presently. Keep out of the circle, I say, lest I
send you into the ostry with a vengeance.

DICK

That's like, 'faith. You had best leave your foolery, for an my master
come, he'll conjure you i'faith.

ROBIN

My master conjure me? I'll tell thee what, an my master come here,   15
I'll clap as fair a pair of horns on's head as ere thou saw'st in thy life.

DICK

Thou needst not do that, for my mistress hath done it.

ROBIN

Ay, there be of us here that have waded as deep into matters as
other men, if they were disposed to talk.

DICK

A plague take you. I thought you did not sneak up and down after   20
her for nothing. But I prithee tell me, in good sadness Robin, is
that a conjuring book?

ROBIN

Do but speak what thou't have me to do, and I'll do't! If thou't
dance naked, put off thy clothes and I'll conjure thee about
presently. Or if thou't go but to the tavern with me, I'll give thee   25
white wine, red wine, claret wine, sack, muscadine, malmesy,
and whippincrust – hold belly hold – and we'll not pay one penny
for it.

DICK

O brave! Prithee let's to it presently, for I am as dry as a dog.

ROBIN

Come then, let's away.   30

Exeunt

[Scene 8]

[*From line 48*]

MEPHOSTOPHILIS

Nay stay my Faustus, I know you'd see the pope
And take some part of holy Peter's feast,
The which this day with high solemnity,   50
This day is held through Rome and Italy,
In honour of the pope's triumphant victory.

FAUSTUS

Sweet Mephostophilis, thou pleasest me.
Whilst I am here on earth, let me be cloyed
With all things that delight the heart of man.   55
My four and twenty years of liberty
I'll spend in pleasure and in dalliance,
That Faustus' name, whilst this bright frame doth stand,
May be admired through the furthest land.

MEPHOSTOPHILIS

'Tis well said Faustus; come then, stand by me,   60
And thou shalt see them come immediately.

FAUSTUS

Nay, stay, my gentle Mephostophilis,
And grant me my request, and then I go.
Thou know'st within the compass of eight days
We view'd the face of heaven, of earth and hell.   65
So high our dragons soar'd into the air,
That looking down the earth appeared to me,
No bigger than my hand in quantity.

There did we view the kingdoms of the world,
And what might please mine eye, I there beheld.   70
Then in this show let me an actor be,
That this proud pope may Faustus' coming see.
MEPHOSTOPHILIS
Let it be so, my Faustus, but first stay,
And view their triumphs, as they pass this way.
And then devise what best contents thy mind,   75
By cunning in thine art to cross the pope,
Or dash the pride of this solemnity;
To make his monks and abbots stand like apes,
And point like antics at his triple crown:
To beat the beads about the friars' pates,   80
Or clap huge horns upon the cardinals' heads:
Or any villainy thou canst devise,
And I'll perform it Faustus: hark, they come:
This day shall make thee be admired in Rome.

Enter the CARDINALS *and Bishops, some bearing croziers, some
the pillars; monks and friars singing their procession.
Then the* POPE *and* RAYMOND *King of Hungary,
with* BRUNO *led in chains*

POPE
Cast down our footstool.
RAYMOND   Saxon Bruno stoop,   85
Whilst on thy back his holiness ascends
Saint Peter's chair and state pontifical.
BRUNO
Proud Lucifer, that state belongs to me:
But thus I fall to Peter, not to thee.
POPE
To me and Peter, shalt thou grovelling lie,   90
And crouch before the papal dignity.
Sound trumpets then, for thus Saint Peter's heir,
From Bruno's back ascends Saint Peter's chair.

A flourish while he ascends

Thus, as the gods, creep on with feet of wool,
Long ere with iron hands they punish men,   95
So shall our sleeping vengeance now arise,

And smite with death thy hated enterprise.
Lord cardinals of France and Padua,
Go forthwith to our holy consistory,
And read amongst the statutes decretal,   100
What by the holy council held at Trent,
The sacred synod hath decreed for him,
That doth assume the papal government,
Without election, and a true consent:
Away and bring us word with speed.   105

1 CARDINAL

We go my Lord.   *Exeunt* CARDINALS

POPE

Lord Raymond.

FAUSTUS

Go haste thee, gentle Mephostophilis,
Follow the cardinals to the consistory;
And as they turn their superstitious books,   110
Strike them with sloth, and drowsy idleness;
And make them sleep so sound, that, in their shapes,
Thyself and I may parley with this pope,
This proud confronter of the emperor;
And in despite of all his holiness   115
Restore this Bruno to his liberty,
And bear him to the states of Germany.

MEPHOSTOPHILIS

Faustus, I go.

FAUSTUS

Dispatch it soon,
The pope shall curse that Faustus came to Rome.   120
                    Exeunt FAUSTUS *and* MEPHOSTOPHILIS

BRUNO

Pope Adrian let me have some right of law,
I was elected by the emperor.

POPE

We will depose the emperor for that deed,
And curse the people that submit to him;
Both he and thou shalt stand excommunicate,   125
And interdict from church's privilege,
And all society of holy men:
He grows too proud in his authority,
Lifting his lofty head above the clouds,

And like a steeple overpeers the church.   130
But we'll pull down his haughty insolence:
And as pope Alexander our progenitor,
Trod on the neck of German Frederick,
Adding this golden sentence to our praise:
That Peter's heirs should tread on emperors,   135
And walk upon the dreadful adder's back,
Treading the lion and the dragon down,
And fearless spurn the killing basilisk:
So will we quell that haughty schismatic,
And by authority apostolical   140
Depose him from his regal government.

BRUNO

Pope Julius swore to princely Sigismond,
For him, and the succeeding popes of Rome,
To hold the emperors their lawful lords.

POPE

Pope Julius did abuse the church's rites,   145
And therefore none of his decrees can stand.
Is not all power on earth bestowed on us?
And therefore tho' we would we cannot err.
Behold this silver belt whereto is fixed
Seven golden seals fast sealed with seven seals,   150
In token of our seven-fold power from heaven,
To bind or loose, lock fast, condemn, or judge,
Resign, or seal, or what so pleaseth us.
Then he and thou, and all the world shall stoop,
Or be assured of our dreadful curse,   155
To light as heavy as the pains of hell.

Enter FAUSTUS *and* MEPHOSTOPHILIS *like the Cardinals*

MEPHOSTOPHILIS

Now tell me Faustus, are we not fitted well?

FAUSTUS

Yes Mephostophilis, and two such cardinals
Ne'er served a holy pope, as we shall do.
But whilst they sleep within the consistory,   160
Let us salute his reverend fatherhood.

RAYMOND

Behold my lord, the cardinals are returned.

91

POPE

    Welcome grave fathers, answer presently,
    What have our holy council there decreed,
    Concerning Bruno and the emperor,   165
    In quittance of their late conspiracy
    Against our state and papal dignity?

FAUSTUS

    Most sacred patron of the church of Rome,
    By full consent of all the synod
    Of priests and prelates, it is thus decreed: 170
    That Bruno, and the German emperor
    Be held as lollards, and bold schismatics,
    And proud disturbers of the church's peace.
    And if that Bruno by his own assent,
    Without enforcement of the German peers,   175
    Did seek to wear the triple diadem,
    And by your death to climb Saint Peter's chair,
    The statutes decretal have thus decreed,
    He shall be straight condemned of heresy,
    And on a pile of faggots burned to death.   180

POPE

    It is enough. Here, take him to your charge,
    And bear him straight to Ponte Angelo,
    And in the strongest tower enclose him fast.
    Tomorrow, sitting in our consistory,
    With all our college of grave cardinals,   185
    We will determine of his life or death.
    Here, take his triple crown along with you,
    And leave it in the church's treasury.
    Make haste again, my good lord cardinals,
    And take our blessing apostolical.   190

MEPHOSTOPHILIS

    So, so, was never devil thus blest before!

FAUSTUS

    Away, sweet Mephostophilis, be gone!
    The cardinals will be plagued for this anon.
                Exeunt FAUSTUS *and* MEPHOSTOPHILIS

POPE

    Go presently, and bring a banquet forth,
    That we may solemnize Saint Peter's feast,   195

And with Lord Raymond, King of Hungary,
Drink to our late and happy victory.   *Exeunt*

A sennet while the banquet is brought in; and then enter
FAUSTUS *and* MEPHOSTOPHILIS *in their*
own shapes

MEPHOSTOPHILIS
Now Faustus, come prepare thyself for mirth;
The sleepy cardinals are hard at hand,
To censure Bruno, that is posted hence,   200
And on a proud paced steed, as swift as thought,
Flies o'er the alps to fruitful Germany,
There to salute the woeful emperor.

FAUSTUS
The pope will curse them for their sloth today
That slept both Bruno and his crown away.   205
But now, that Faustus may delight his mind,
And by their folly make some merriment,
Sweet Mephostophilis, so charm me here,
That I may walk invisible to all,
And do whate'er I please, unseen of any.   210

MEPHOSTOPHILIS
Faustus thou shalt; then kneel down presently,
Whilst on thy head I lay my hand,
And charm thee with this magic wand.
First wear this girdle, then appear
Invisible to all are here: 215
The planets seven, the gloomy air,
Hell, and the Fury's forked hair,
Pluto's blue fire, and Hecate's tree,
With magic spells so compass thee,
That no eye may thy body see.   220
So Faustus, now for all their holiness,
Do what thou wilt, thou shalt not be discerned.

FAUSTUS
Thanks Mephostophilis; now friars, take heed
Lest Faustus make your shaven crowns to bleed.

MEPHOSTOPHILIS
Faustus, no more: see where the cardinals come.   225

Enter POPE *and all the lords. Enter the* CARDINALS *with a book*

93

POPE

    Welcome lord cardinals: come sit down.

    Lord Raymond, take your seat; friars, attend,

    And see that all things be in readiness,

    As beseems this solemn festival.

1 CARDINAL

    First, may it please your sacred holiness   230

    To view the sentence of the reverend synod,

    Concerning Bruno and the emperor.

POPE

    What needs this question? Did I not tell you,

    Tomorrow we would sit i'th' consistory,

    And there determine of his punishment?   235

    You brought us word even now, it was decreed,

    That Bruno and the cursed emperor

    Were by the holy council both condemned

    For loathed lollards, and base schismatics.

    Then wherefore would you have me view that book?   240

1 CARDINAL

    Your grace mistakes, you gave us no such charge.

RAYMOND

    Deny it not, we all are witnesses

    That Bruno here was late delivered you,

    With his rich triple crown to be reserved

    And put into the church's treasury.   245

AMBO CARDINALS

    By holy Paul we saw them not.

POPE

    By Peter you shall die,

    Unless you bring them forth immediately:

    Hale them to prison, lade their limbs with gyves!

    False prelates, for this hateful treachery,   250

    Cursed be your souls to hellish misery.

FAUSTUS

    So, they are safe: now Faustus to the feast,

    The pope had never such a frolic guest.

POPE

    Lord archbishop of Rheims, sit down with us.

BISHOP

    I thank your holiness.   255

FAUSTUS

Fall to, the devil choke you an you spare.

POPE

Who's that spoke? Friars, look about.
Lord Raymond pray fall to; I am beholding
To the bishop of Milan for this so rare a present.

FAUSTUS

I thank you sir.   260

POPE

How now? Who snatched the meat from me?
Villains, why speak you not?
My good lord archbishop, here's a most dainty dish,
Was sent me from a cardinal in France.

FAUSTUS

I'll have that too.   265

POPE

What lollards do attend our holiness
That we receive such great indignity? Fetch me some wine.

FAUSTUS

Ay, pray do, for Faustus is a-dry.

POPE

Lord Raymond, I drink unto your grace.

FAUSTUS

I pledge your grace.   270

POPE

My wine gone too? Ye lubbers, look about
And find the man that doth this villainy,
Or by our sanctitude you all shall die.
I pray my lords, have patience at this
Troublesome banquet.   275

BISHOP

Please it your holiness, I think it be some ghost crept out of
purgatory, and now is come unto your holiness for his pardon.

POPE

It may be so:
Go then command our priests to sing a dirge,
To lay the fury of this same troublesome ghost.   280

FAUSTUS

How now? Must every bit be spiced with a cross?
Nay then, take that.

POPE

    O I am slain, help me my lords;

    O come and help to bear my body hence.

    Damned be this soul for ever, for this deed.   285

                    Exeunt the POPE *and his train*

MEPHOSTOPHILIS

    Now Faustus, what will you do now? for I can tell you

    You'll be cursed with bell, book and candle.

FAUSTUS

    Bell, book, and candle; candle, book, and bell:

    Forward and backward, to curse Faustus to hell.

        Enter the FRIARS *with bell, book, and candle,*
                for the dirge

1 FRIAR

    Come brethren, let's about our business with good devotion.   290

        Cursed be he that stole his holiness' meat from the table.

                Maledicat Dominus.

        Cursed be he that struck his holiness a blow [on] the face.

                Maledicat Dominus.

        Cursed be he that struck friar Sandelo a blow on the pate.   295

                Maledicat Dominus.

        Cursed be he that disturbeth our holy dirge.

                Maledicat Dominus.

        Cursed be he that took away his holiness' wine

                Maledicat Dominus.   300

        Beat the FRIARS, *fling fireworks among them,*
                and exeunt

                            Exeunt

[Scene 9]

      Enter CLOWN [ROBIN] *and* DICK, *with a cup*

DICK

    Sirra Robin, we were best look that your devil can answer the
    stealing of this same cup, for the vintner's boy follows us at the
    hard heels.

ROBIN

    'Tis no matter, let him come; an he follow us, I'll so conjure him, as
    he was never conjured in his life, I warrant him. Let me see the cup.   5

Enter VINTNER

DICK

Here 'tis. Yonder he comes: now Robin, now or never show thy
cunning.

VINTNER

O, are you here? I am glad I have found you, you are a couple of
fine companions: pray where's the cup you stole from the tavern?

ROBIN

How, how? We steal a cup? Take heed what you say, we look not   10
like cup-stealers, I can tell you.

VINTNER

Never deny't, for I know you have it, and I'll search you.

ROBIN

Search me? Ay, and spare not: hold the cup Dick – come, come,
search me, search me.

VINTNER

Come on sirra, let me search you now.   15

DICK

Ay, ay; do, do. Hold the cup, Robin. I fear not your searching; we
scorn to steal your cups, I can tell you.

VINTNER

Never outface me for the matter, for sure the cup is between you
two.

ROBIN

Nay there you lie, 'tis beyond us both.   20

VINTNER

A plague take you, I thought 'twas your knavery to take it away.
Come, give it me again.

ROBIN

Ay, much, when can you tell? Dick, make me a circle and stand
close at my back, and stir not for thy life. Vintner, you shall have
your cup anon – say nothing, Dick. *O per se o, demogorgon, Belcher* 25
and *Mephostophilis*.

Enter MEPHOSTOPHILIS

MEPHOSTOPHILIS

You princely legions of infernal rule,
How am I vexed by these villains' charms?
From Constantinople have they brought me now,
Only for pleasure of these damned slaves.   30

ROBIN

By lady sir, you have had a shrewd journey of it! Will it please you
to take a shoulder of mutton to supper, and a tester in your purse,
and go back again?

DICK

Ay, I pray you heartily sir, for we called you but in jest, I promise
you.   35

MEPHOSTOPHILIS

To purge the rashness of this cursed deed,
First, be thou turned to this ugly shape,
For apish deeds transformed to an ape.

ROBIN

O brave, an ape? I pray sir, let me have the carrying of him about
to show some tricks.   40

MEPHOSTOPHILIS

And so thou shalt: be thou transformed to a dog, and carry him
upon thy back. Away, be gone.

ROBIN

A dog? That's excellent: let the maids look well to their porridge-
pots, for I'll into the kitchen presently. Come Dick, come.

Exeunt the two CLOWNS

MEPHOSTOPHILIS

Now with the flames of ever-burning fire,   45
I'll wing my self, and forthwith fly amain
Unto my Faustus, to the great Turk's court.   *Exit*

[Scene 10]

Enter MARTINO *and* FREDERICK *at several doors*

MARTINO

What ho, officers, gentlemen,
Hie to the presence to attend the emperor.
Good Frederick, see the rooms be voided straight;
His majesty is coming to the hall;
Go back, and see the state in readiness.   5

FREDERICK

But where is Bruno, our elected pope,
That on a Fury's back came post from Rome?
Will not his grace consort the emperor?

MARTINO

    O yes; and with him comes the German conjuror,

    The learned Faustus, fame of Wittenberg,   10

    The wonder of the world for magic art.

    And he intends to show great Carolus

    The race of all his stout progenitors;

    And bring in presence of his majesty

    The royal shapes and warlike semblances   15

    Of Alexander and his beauteous paramour.

FREDERICK

    Where is Benvolio?

MARTINO

    Fast asleep, I warrant you;

    He took his rouse with stoops of Rhenish wine

    So kindly yesternight to Bruno's health,   20

    That all this day the sluggard keeps his bed.

FREDERICK

    See, see – his window's ope; we'll call to him.

MARTINO

    What ho, Benvolio!

Enter BENVOLIO *above at a window,*
in his nightcap: buttoning

BENVOLIO

    What a devil ail you two?

MARTINO

    Speak softly sir, lest the devil hear you: 25

    For Faustus at the court is late arrived,

    And at his heels a thousand furies wait

    To accomplish whatsoever the doctor please.

BENVOLIO

    What of this?

MARTINO

    Come, leave thy chamber first, and thou shalt see   30

    This conjuror perform such rare exploits

    Before the pope and royal emperor,

    As never yet was seen in Germany.

BENVOLIO

    Has not the pope enough of conjuring yet?

    35

He was upon the devil's back late enough,
And if he be so far in love with him,
I would he would post with him to Rome again.

FREDERICK
Speak, wilt thou come and see this sport?

BENVOLIO
Not I.

MARTINO
Wilt thou stand in thy window and see it then?   40

BENVOLIO
Ay, and I fall not asleep i'th' meantime.

MARTINO
The emperor is at hand, who comes to see
What wonders by black spells may compassed be.

BENVOLIO
Well, go you attend the emperor. I am content for this once to
thrust my head out at a window – for they say, if a man be drunk   45
overnight, the devil cannot hurt him in the morning. If that be
true, I have a charm in my head, shall control him as well as the
conjuror, I warrant you.   [*Withdraws*]

A sennet. [*Enter*] CHARLES *the German emperor,* BRUNO,
SAXONY, FAUSTUS, MEPHOSTOPHILIS,
[*to*] FREDERICK, MARTINO, *and Attendants*

EMPEROR
Wonder of men, renowned magician,
Thrice learned Faustus, welcome to our court.   50
This deed of thine, in setting Bruno free
From his and our professed enemy,
Shall add more excellence unto thine art
Than if by powerful necromantic spells
Thou couldst command the world's obedience: 55
For ever be beloved of Carolus.
And if this Bruno thou hast late redeemed
In peace possess the triple diadem,
And sit in Peter's chair, despite of chance,
Thou shalt be famous through all Italy,   60
And honoured of the German emperor.

FAUSTUS
These gracious words, most royal Carolus,

Shall make poor Faustus to his utmost power
Both love and serve the German emperor,
And lay his life at holy Bruno's feet.   65
For proof whereof, if so your grace be pleased,
The doctor stands prepared, by power of art,
To cast his magic charms, that shall pierce through
The ebon gates of ever-burning hell,
And hale the stubborn Furies from their caves,   70
To compass whatso'er your grace commands.

BENVOLIO [Above]
'Blood, he speaks terribly! But for all that, I do not greatly believe
him: he looks as like conjuror as the pope to a costermonger.

EMPEROR
Then Faustus, as thou late didst promise us,
We would behold that famous conqueror,   75
Great Alexander, and his paramour,
In their true shapes and state majestical,
That we may wonder at their excellence.

FAUSTUS
Your majesty shall see them presently.
Mephostophilis, away,   80
And with a solemn noise of trumpets' sound,
Present before this royal emperor,
Great Alexander and his beauteous paramour.

MEPHOSTOPHILIS
Faustus I will.

BENVOLIO
Well master doctor, an your devils come not away quickly, you   85
shall have me asleep presently: zounds, I could eat myself for anger,
to think I have been such an ass all this while, to stand gaping after
the devil's governor, and can see nothing.

FAUSTUS
I'll make you feel something anon, if my art fail me not.
My lord, I must forewarn your majesty   90
That when my spirits present the royal shapes
Of Alexander and his paramour,
Your grace demand no questions of the king,
But in dumb silence let them come and go.

EMPEROR
Be it as Faustus please, we are content.   95

BENVOLIO

Ay, ay; and I am content too: and thou bring Alexander and his
paramour before the emperor, I'll be Actaeon, and turn myself
into a stag.

FAUSTUS

And I'll play Diana, and send you the horns presently.

> *Sennet. Enter at one [door] the emperor* ALEXANDER,
> *at the other [door]* DARIUS; *they meet,* DARIUS *is thrown
> down,* ALEXANDER *kills him, takes off his crown, and
> offering to go out, his paramour meets him. He embraceth
> her, and sets Darius' crown upon her head; and coming
> back, both salute the emperor who, leaving his state, offers to
> embrace them, which* FAUSTUS *seeing, suddenly stays him.
> Then trumpets cease, and music sounds*

My gracious lord, you do forget yourself: 100
These are but shadows, not substantial.

EMPEROR

O pardon me, my thoughts are so ravished
With sight of this renowned emperor,
That in mine arms I would have compassed him.
But Faustus, since I may not speak to them,   105
To satisfy my longing thoughts at full,
Let me this tell thee: I have heard it said,
That this fair lady, whilst she lived on earth,
Had on her neck a little wart or mole;
How may I prove that saying to be true?   110

FAUSTUS

Your majesty may boldly go and see.

EMPEROR

Faustus, I see it plain!
And in this sight thou better pleasest me,
Than if I gained another monarchy.

FAUSTUS

Away, be gone.   *Exit Show*   115
See, see, my gracious lord, what strange beast is yon, that thrusts
his head out at window.

EMPEROR

O wondrous sight: see, duke of Saxony,
Two spreading horns most strangely fastened
Upon the head of young Benvolio.   120

SAXONY
What, is he asleep – or dead?

FAUSTUS
He sleeps, my lord, but dreams not of his horns.

EMPEROR
This sport is excellent: we'll call and wake him.
What ho, Benvolio!

BENVOLIO
A plague upon you, let me sleep awhile.   125

EMPEROR
I blame thee not to sleep much, having such a head of thine
own.

SAXONY
Look up, Benvolio; 'tis the emperor calls.

BENVOLIO
The emperor! Where? O zounds, my head.

EMPEROR
Nay, and thy horns hold, 'tis no matter for thy head, for that's   130
armed sufficiently.

FAUSTUS
Why, how now sir knight, what hanged by the horns? This [is]
most horrible: fie, fie, pull in your head for shame, let not all the
world wonder at you.

BENVOLIO
Zounds, doctor, is this your villainy?   135

FAUSTUS
O say not so, sir: the doctor has no skill,
No art, no cunning, to present these lords,
Or bring before this royal emperor
The mighty monarch, warlike Alexander.
If Faustus do it, you are straight resolved   140
In bold Actaeon's shape to turn a stag.
And therefore, my lord – so please your majesty –
I'll raise a kennel of hounds shall hunt him so
As all his footmanship shall scarce prevail
To keep his carcass from their bloody fangs.   145
Ho, Belimoth, Argiron, Asteroth!

BENVOLIO
Hold, hold! Zounds, he'll raise up a kennel of devils, I think, anon.
Good my lord, entreat for me: 'sblood, I am never able to endure
these torments.

EMPEROR

Then, good master doctor,   150
Let me entreat you to remove his horns:
He has done penance now sufficiently.

FAUSTUS

My gracious lord, not so much for injury done to me, as to delight
your majesty with some mirth, hath Faustus justly requited this
injurious knight; which being all I desire, I am content to remove   155
his horns. Mephostophilis, transform him; and hereafter sir, look
you speak well of scholars.

BENVOLIO

Speak well of you? 'Sblood, and scholars be such cuckold-makers
to clap horns of honest men's heads o'this order. I'll ne'er trust
smooth faces and small ruffs more. But an I be not revenged for   160
this, would I might be turned to a gaping oyster and drink nothing
but salt water.   [*Exit*]

EMPEROR

Come Faustus; while the emperor lives,
In recompence of this thy high desert,
Thou shalt command the state of Germany,   165
And live beloved of mighty Carolus.

Exeunt omnes

[Scene 10b]

Enter BENVOLIO, MARTINO, FREDERICK, *and* SOLDIERS

MARTINO

Nay, sweet Benvolio, let us sway thy thoughts
From this attempt against the conjuror.

BENVOLIO

Away, you love me not to urge me thus.
Shall I let slip so great an injury,   170
When every servile groom jests at my wrongs,
And in their rustic gambols proudly say,
'Benvolio's head was graced with horns today'!
O may these eyelids never close again,
Till with my sword I have that conjuror slain.   175
If you will aid me in this enterprise,
Then draw your weapons, and be resolute:
If not, depart: here will Benvolio die –

But Faustus' death shall quit my infamy!

FREDERICK

Nay, we will stay with thee, betide what may,   180
And kill that doctor if he come this way.

BENVOLIO

Then gentle Frederick, hie thee to the grove,
And place our servants, and our followers
Close in an ambush there behind the trees;
By this (I know) the conjuror is near: 185
I saw him kneel, and kiss the emperor's hand,
And take his leave, laden with rich rewards.
Then soldiers, boldly fight; if Faustus die,
Take you the wealth, leave us the victory.

FREDERICK

Come soldiers, follow me unto the grove;   190
Who kills him shall have gold, and endless love.

Exit FREDERICK *with the* SOLDIERS

BENVOLIO

My head is lighter than it was by th'horns,
But yet my heart more ponderous than my head,
And pants until I see that conjuror dead.

MARTINO

Where shall we place ourselves Benvolio?   195

BENVOLIO

Here will we stay to bide the first assault.
O were that damned hellhound but in place,
Thou soon shouldst see me quit my foul disgrace.

Enter FREDERICK

FREDERICK

Close, close, the conjuror is at hand,
And, all alone, comes walking in his gown.   200
Be ready then, and strike the peasant down.

BENVOLIO

Mine be that honour then: now sword strike home,
For horns he gave, I'll have his head anon.

Enter FAUSTUS *with the false head*

MARTINO

See, see, he comes.

BENVOLIO

No words: this blow ends all! 205

[They attack FAUSTUS]

Hell take his soul, his body thus must fall.

FAUSTUS

Oh.

FREDERICK

Groan you, master doctor?

BENVOLIO

Break may his heart with groans! Dear Frederick, see

Thus will I end his griefs immediately. 210

MARTINO

Strike with a willing hand, his head is off.

BENVOLIO

The devil's dead, the furies now may laugh.

FREDERICK

Was this that stern aspect, that awful frown,

Made the grim monarch of infernal spirits

Tremble and quake at his commanding charms? 215

MARTINO

Was this that damned head, whose heart conspired

Benvolio's shame before the emperor?

BENVOLIO

Ay that's the head, and here the body lies,

Justly rewarded for his villainies.

FREDERICK

Come, let's devise how we may add more shame 220

To the black scandal of his hated name.

BENVOLIO

First, on his head, in quittance of my wrongs,

I'll nail huge forked horns, and let them hang

Within the window where he yoked me first,

That all the world may see my just revenge. 225

MARTINO

What use shall we put his beard to?

BENVOLIO

We'll sell it to a chimney-sweeper: it will wear out ten birchen

brooms, I warrant you.

FREDERICK

What shall eyes do?

BENVOLIO

We'll put out his eyes, and they shall serve for buttons to his lips, 230
to keep his tongue from catching cold.

MARTINO

An excellent policy! And now sirs, having divided him, what shall
the body do?

[FAUSTUS *gets up*]

BENVOLIO

Zounds, the devil's alive again.

FREDERICK

Give him his head, for God's sake. 235

FAUSTUS

Nay keep it: Faustus will have heads and hands,
Ay, all your hearts to recompense this deed.
Knew you not, traitors, I was limited
For four-and-twenty years to breathe on earth?
And had you cut my body with your swords, 240
Or hew'd this flesh and bones as small as sand,
Yet in a minute had my spirit returned,
And I had breathed a man made free from harm.
But wherefore do I dally my revenge?
Asteroth, Belimoth, Mephostophilis. 245

Enter MEPHOSTOPHILIS *and other* DEVILS

Go, horse these traitors on your fiery backs,
And mount aloft with them as high as heaven,
Thence pitch them headlong to the lowest hell:
Yet stay, the world shall see their misery,
And hell shall after plague their treachery. 250
Go Belimoth, and take this caitiff hence,
And hurl him in some lake of mud and dirt;
Take thou this other, drag him through the woods,
Amongst the pricking thorns and sharpest briars,
Whilst with my gentle Mephostophilis, 255
This traitor flies unto some steepy rock,
That rolling down, may break the villain's bones,
As he intended to dismember me.
Fly hence, dispatch my charge immediately.

FREDERICK
Pity us, gentle Faustus, save our lives. 260
FAUSTUS
Away.
FREDERICK
He must needs go that the devil drives.

Exeunt SPIRITS *with the* KNIGHTS

Enter the ambushed SOLDIERS

1 SOLDIER
Come sirs, prepare yourselves in readiness,
Make haste to help these noble gentlemen.
I heard them parley with the conjuror. 265
2 SOLDIER
See where he comes! Dispatch, and kill the slave.
FAUSTUS
What's here? An ambush to betray my life!
Then Faustus, try thy skill: base peasants stand,
For lo, these trees remove at my command,
And stand as bulwarks 'twixt yourselves and me, 270
To shield me from your hated treachery!
Yet to encounter this your weak attempt,
Behold an army comes incontinent.

FAUSTUS *strikes the door, and enter a* DEVIL *playing
on a drum; after him another bearing an ensign; and
divers with weapons,* MEPHOSTOPHILIS *with fireworks.
They set upon the* SOLDIERS, *and drive them out*

Enter at several doors BENVOLIO, FREDERICK, *and* MARTINO,
*their heads and faces bloody, and besmeared with
mud and dirt; all having horns on their heads*

MARTINO
What ho, Benvolio!
BENVOLIO
Here, what Frederick, ho! 275
FREDERICK
O help me, gentle friend; where is Martino?

MARTINO
    Dear Frederick, here –
    Half smothered in a lake of mud and dirt,
    Through which the Furies dragged me by the heels.

FREDERICK
    Martino, see   280
    Benvolio's horns again!

MARTINO
    O misery! How now Benvolio?

BENVOLIO
    Defend me heaven, shall I be haunted still?

MARTINO
    Nay fear not, man; we have no power to kill.

BENVOLIO
    My friends transformed thus: O hellish spite,   285
    Your heads are all set with horns.

FREDERICK   You hit it right,
    It is your own you mean: feel on your head.

BENVOLIO
    'Zounds, horns again!

MARTINO
    Nay chafe not, man: we all are sped.

BENVOLIO
    What devil attends this damned magician,   290
    That spite of spite our wrongs are doubled?

FREDERICK
    What may we do, that we may hide our shames?

BENVOLIO
    If we should follow him to work revenge,
    He'd join long asses' ears to these huge horns,
    And make us laughing-stocks to all the world.   295

MARTINO
    What shall we do then, dear Benvolio?

BENVOLIO
    I have a castle joining near these woods,
    And thither we'll repair, and live obscure
    Till time shall alter this our brutish shapes.
    Sith black disgrace hath thus eclipsed our fame, 300
    We'll rather die with grief, than live with shame.

                                  Exeunt omnes

[Scene 10c]

[This is a new scene in the B-text, and not a continuation of Scene 10, as in the A-text]

Enter FAUSTUS *and the* HORSE-COURSER, *and* MEPHOSTOPHILIS

HORSE-COURSER

I beseech your worship accept of these forty dollars.

FAUSTUS

Friend, thou canst not buy so good a horse, for so small a price:
I have no great need to sell him, but if thou likest him for ten
dollars more, take him, because I see thou hast a good mind to
him. 5

HORSE-COURSER

I beseech you sir, accept of this; I am a very poor man, and have
lost very much of late by horseflesh, and this bargain will set me
up again.

FAUSTUS

Well, I will not stand with thee; give me the money. Now sirra I must
tell you, that you may ride him o'er hedge and ditch, and spare him 10
not; but, do you hear, in any case ride him not into the water.

HORSE-COURSER

How sir, not into the water? Why, will he not drink of all waters?

FAUSTUS

Yes, he will drink of all waters, but ride him not into the water:
o'er hedge and ditch, or where thou wilt, but not into the water.
Go bid the ostler deliver him unto you, and remember what I say. 15

HORSE-COURSER

I warrant you sir. O joyful day! Now am I a made man for ever.

Exit

FAUSTUS

What art thou, Faustus, but a man condemned to die?
Thy fatal time draws to a final end;
Despair doth drive distrust into my thoughts.
Confound these passions with a quiet sleep: 20
Tush, Christ did call the thief upon the cross,
Then rest thee, Faustus, quiet in conceit.

He sits to sleep

Enter the HORSE-COURSER *wet*

HORSE-COURSER

O what a cozening doctor was this! I riding my horse into the water, thinking some hidden mystery had been in the horse, I had nothing under me but a little straw, and had much ado to escape 25 drowning! Well, I'll go rouse him, and make him give me my forty dollars again. Ho, sirra doctor, you cozening scab; master doctor awake, and rise, and give me my money again, for your horse is turned to a bottle of hay, – master doctor.

He pulls off his leg

Alas I am undone, what shall I do? I have pulled off his leg.   30

FAUSTUS

O help, help, the villain hath murdered me.

HORSE-COURSER

Murder or not murder, now he has but one leg, I'll out-run him, and cast this leg into some ditch or other.   *Exit*

FAUSTUS

Stop him, stop him, stop him – ha, ha, ha, Faustus hath his leg again, and the horse-courser a bundle of hay for his forty dollars.   35

Enter WAGNER

How now Wagner, what news with thee?

WAGNER

If it please you, the Duke of Vanholt doth earnestly entreat your company, and hath sent some of his men to attend you with provision fit for your journey.

FAUSTUS

The Duke of Vanholt's an honourable gentleman, and one to   40 whom I must be no niggard of my cunning. Come away.

Exeunt

[Scene 10d]

[This scene is found only the B-text, where it follows Scene 10c]

Enter CLOWN [ROBIN], DICK, HORSE-COURSER
and a CARTER

CARTER

Come, my masters, I'll bring you to the best beer in Europe. What ho, hostess, where be these whores?

Enter HOSTESS

HOSTESS

How now, what lack you? What, my old guests, welcome.

ROBIN

Sirra Dick, dost thou know why I stand so mute?

DICK

No Robin, why is't?   5

ROBIN

I am eighteen pence on the score, but say nothing, see if she have forgotten me.

HOSTESS

Who's this, that stands so solemnly by himself? What, my old guest?

ROBIN

O hostess, how do you? I hope my score stands still.   10

HOSTESS

Ay, there's no doubt of that, for methinks you make no haste to wipe it out.

DICK

Why hostess, I say, fetch us some beer.

HOSTESS

You shall presently: look up into th'hall there, ho!   *Exit*

DICK

Come sirs, what shall we do now till mine hostess comes?   15

CARTER

Marry sir, I'll tell you the bravest tale how a conjuror served me; you know Doctor Fauster?

HORSE-COURSER

Ay, a plague take him! Here's some on's have cause to know him; did he conjure thee too?

CARTER

I'll tell you how he served me. As I was going to Wittenberg t'other   20
day, with a load of hay, he met me, and asked me what he should
give me for as much hay as he could eat; now sir, I thinking that
a little would serve his turn, bade him take as much as he would
for three-farthings; so he presently gave me my money, and fell
to eating; and as I am a christen man, he never left eating, till he   25
had ate up all my load of hay.

ALL

O monstrous, eat a whole load of hay!

ROBIN

Yes, yes, that may be; for I have heard of one, that ha's ate a load of logs.

HORSE-COURSER

Now sirs, you shall hear how villainously he served me: I went to   30
him yesterday to buy a horse of him, and he would by no means
sell him under forty dollars; so sir, because I knew him to be such
a horse, as would run over hedge and ditch, and never tire, I gave
him his money; so when I had my horse, Doctor Fauster bade me
ride him night and day, and spare him no time; but, quoth he, in   35
any case ride him not into the water. Now sir, I thinking the horse
had had some quality that he would not have me know of, what
did I but rid him into a great river, and when I came just in the
midst my horse vanished away, and I sat straddling upon a bottle
of hay.   40

ALL

O brave, doctor!

HORSE-COURSER

But you shall hear how bravely I served him for it. I went me
home to his house, and there I found him asleep. I kept a hallowing
and whooping in his ears, but all could not wake him; I, seeing
that, took him by the leg, and never rested pulling, till I had pulled   45
me his leg quite off, and now 'tis at home in mine hostry.

ROBIN

And has the doctor but one leg then? That's excellent, for one of
his devils turned me into the likeness of an ape's face.

CARTER

Some more drink, hostess.

ROBIN

Hark you, we'll into another room and drink awhile, and then   50
we'll go seek out the doctor.

Exeunt omnes

[Scene 11]

Enter the DUKE *of Vanholt; his* DUCHESS,
FAUSTUS, *and* MEPHOSTOPHILIS

DUKE

Thanks, master doctor, for these pleasant sights; nor know I how
sufficiently to recompense your great deserts in erecting that
enchanted castle in the air; the sight whereof so delighted me, as

113

nothing in the world could please me more.

FAUSTUS

I do think myself, my good lord, highly recompensed, in that it 5
pleaseth your grace to think but well of that which Faustus hath
performed. But, gracious lady, it may be, that you have taken no
pleasure in those sights; therefore I pray you tell me, what is the thing
you most desire to have: be it in the world, it shall be yours. I have
heard that great-bellied women do long for things are rare and dainty. 10

DUCHESS

True, master doctor; and since I find you so kind I will make known
unto you what my heart desires to have; and were it now summer,
as it is January, a dead time of the winter, I would request no better
meat, than a dish of ripe grapes.

FAUSTUS

This is but a small matter: go Mephostophilis; away! 15

Exit MEPHOSTOPHILIS

Madam, I will do more than this for your content.

Enter MEPHOSTOPHILIS *again with the grapes*

Here now taste ye these: they should be good
For they come from a far country, I can tell you.

DUKE

This makes me wonder more than all the rest, that at this time of
the year, when every tree is barren of his fruit, from whence you 20
had these ripe grapes.

FAUSTUS

Please it your grace, the year is divided into two circles over the
whole world, so that when it is winter with us, in the contrary
circle it is likewise summer with them, as in India, Saba, and such
countries that lie far east, where they have fruit twice a year. From 25
whence, by means of a swift spirit that I have, I had these grapes
brought as you see.

DUCHESS

And trust me, they are the sweetest grapes that e'er I tasted.

The CLOWNS [ROBIN, DICK, CARTER, HORSE-COURSER]
bounce at the gate, within

DUKE

What rude disturbers have we at the gate?

Go pacify their fury, set it ope, 30
And then demand of them, what they would have.

They knock again, and call out to talk with FAUSTUS [*within*]

A SERVANT
Why how now masters, what a coil is there?
What is the reason you disturb the duke?
DICK
We have no reason for it, therefore a fig for him.
SERVANT
Why saucy varlets, dare you be so bold? 35
HORSE-COURSER
I hope sir, we have wit enough to be more bold than welcome.
SERVANT
It appears so. Pray be bold elsewhere,
And trouble not the duke.
DUKE
What would they have?
SERVANT
They all cry out to speak with Doctor Faustus. 40
CARTER
Ay, and we will speak with him.
DUKE
Will you sir? Commit the rascals.
DICK
Commit with us! He were as good commit with his father, as
commit with us.
FAUSTUS
I do beseech your grace let them come in, 45
They are good subject for a merriment.
DUKE
Do as thou wilt Faustus, I give thee leave.
FAUSTUS
I thank your grace:

Enter the CLOWN [ROBIN], DICK, CARTER, *and* HORSE-COURSER

               Why, how now, my good friends?
'Faith you are too outrageous, but come near,
I have procured your pardons: welcome all. 50

ROBIN
> Nay sir, we will be welcome for our money, and we will pay for
> what we take. What ho, give's half a dozen of beer here, and be
> hanged.

FAUSTUS
> Nay, hark you, can you tell me where you are?

CARTER
> Ay, marry can I, we are under heaven. 55

SERVANT
> Ay; but, sir sauce-box, know you in what place?

HORSE-COURSER
> Ay, ay: the house is good enough to drink in. Zounds, fill us some
> beer, or we'll break all the barrels in the house, and dash out all
> your brains with your bottles.

FAUSTUS
> Be not so furious: come, you shall have beer. 60
> My Lord, beseech you give me leave awhile,
> I'll gage my credit, 'twill content your grace.

DUKE
> With all my heart, kind doctor; please thyself,
> Our servants, and our court's at thy command.

FAUSTUS
> I humbly thank your grace: then fetch some beer. 65

HORSE-COURSER
> Ay, marry; there spake a doctor indeed – and 'faith I'll drink a
> health to thy wooden leg for that word.

FAUSTUS
> My wooden leg? what dost thou mean by that?

CARTER
> Ha, ha, ha, dost hear him Dick? He has forgot his leg.

HORSE-COURSER
> Ay, ay, he does not stand much upon that. 70

FAUSTUS
> No 'faith, not much upon a wooden leg.

CARTER
> Good Lord, that flesh and blood should be so frail with your wor-
> ship! Do not you remember a horse-courser you sold a horse to?

FAUSTUS
> Yes, I remember I sold one a horse.

CARTER
> And do you remember you bid he should not ride into the water? 75

FAUSTUS

Yes, I do very well remember that.

CARTER

And do you remember nothing of your leg?

FAUSTUS

No, in good sooth.

CARTER

Then I pray remember your courtesy.

FAUSTUS [*Bowing*]

I thank you sir.   80

CARTER

'Tis not so much worth; I pray you tell me one thing.

FAUSTUS

What's that?

CARTER

Be both your legs bedfellows every night together?

FAUSTUS

Wouldst thou make a colossus of me, that thou askest me such

questions?   85

CARTER

No, truly sir, I would make nothing of you, but I would fain know

that.

Enter HOSTESS *with drink*

FAUSTUS

Then I assure thee certainly they are.

CARTER

I thank you; I am fully satisfied.

FAUSTUS

But wherefore dost thou ask?   90

CARTER

For nothing sir: but methinks you should have a wooden bedfellow

of one of 'em.

HORSE-COURSER

Why, do you hear sir, did not I pull off one of your legs when you

were asleep?

FAUSTUS

But I have it again now I am awake: look you here, sir.   95

ALL

O horrible! Had the doctor three legs?

117

CARTER

Do you remember sir, how you cozened me and eat up my load
of –

FAUSTUS charms him dumb

DICK

Do you remember how you made me wear an ape's –

HORSE-COURSER

You whoreson conjuring scab, do you remember how you cozened   100
me with a ho –

ROBIN

Ha' you forgotten me? You think to carry it away with your hey-
pass and re-pass: do you remember the dog's fa –

Exeunt CLOWNS

HOSTESS

Who pays for the ale – hear you, master doctor, now you have sent
away my guests. I pray who shall pay me for my a –   105

Exit HOSTESS

DUCHESS

My lord,
We are much beholding to this learned man.

DUKE

So are we madam, which we will recompense
With all the love and kindness that we may:
His artful sport drives all sad thoughts away.   110

Exeunt

[Scene 12]

Thunder and lightning. Enter DEVILS *with covered dishes;*
MEPHOSTOPHILIS *leads them into* FAUSTUS' *study*
Then enter WAGNER

WAGNER

I think my master means to die shortly. He has made his will, and
given me his wealth, his house, his goods, and store of golden
plate, besides two thousand ducats ready coined: I wonder what he
means? If death were nigh, he would not frolic thus: he's now at
supper with the scholars, where there's such belly-cheer, as Wagner   5
in his life ne'er saw the like! And see where they come, belike the
feast is done.   *Exit*

Enter FAUSTUS, MEPHOSTOPHILIS,
and two or three SCHOLARS

1 SCHOLAR

Master doctor Faustus, since our conference about fair ladies, which
was the beautifullest in all the world, we have determined
with ourselves, that Helen of Greece was the admirablest lady that   10
ever lived: therefore master doctor, if you will do us so much favour,
as to let us see that peerless dame of Greece, whom all the world
admires for majesty, we should think ourselves much beholding unto
you.

FAUSTUS

Gentlemen, for that I know your friendship is unfained,   15
It is not Faustus' custom to deny
The just request of those that wish him well:
You shall behold that peerless dame of Greece,
No otherwise for pomp or majesty,
Than when sir Paris crossed the seas with her,   20
And brought the spoils to rich Dardania.
Be silent then, for danger is in words.

Music sound. MEPHOSTOPHILIS *brings in* HELEN;
she passeth over the stage

2 SCHOLAR

Was this fair Helen, whose admired worth
Made Greece with ten years' war afflict poor Troy?

3 SCHOLAR

Too simple is my wit to tell her worth,   25
Whom all the world admires for majesty.

1 SCHOLAR

Now we have seen the pride of Nature's work,
We'll take our leaves, and for this blessed sight
Happy and blest be Faustus evermore.

Exeunt SCHOLARS

FAUSTUS

Gentlemen farewell: the same wish I to you.   30

Enter an OLD MAN

OLD MAN

O gentle Faustus, leave this damned art,
This magic, that will charm thy soul to hell,
And quite bereave thee of salvation.

Though thou hast now offended like a man,
Do not persevere in it like a devil. 35
Yet, yet, thou hast an amiable soul,
If sin by custom grow not into nature.
Then Faustus, will repentance come too late,
Then thou art banished from the sight of heaven.
No mortal can express the pains of hell! 40
It may be this my exhortation
Seems harsh, and all unpleasant; let it not,
For, gentle son, I speak it not in wrath,
Or envy of thee, but in tender love,
And pity of thy future misery. 45
And so have hope, that this my kind rebuke,
Checking thy body, may amend thy soul.

FAUSTUS

Where art thou, Faustus? wretch, what hast thou done?
Hell claims his right, and with a roaring voice,

MEPHOSTOPHILIS *gives him a dagger*

Says 'Faustus, come: thine hour is almost come'; 50
And Faustus now will come to do thee right.

OLD MAN

O stay, good Faustus, stay thy desperate steps.
I see an angel hover o'er thy head,
And with a vial full of precious grace,
Offers to pour the same into thy soul! 55
Then call for mercy, and avoid despair.

FAUSTUS

O friend, I feel thy words to comfort my distressed soul!
Leave me awhile, to ponder on my sins.

OLD MAN

Faustus I leave thee, but with grief of heart,
Fearing the enemy of thy hapless soul. *Exit* 60

FAUSTUS

Accursed Faustus, wretch, what hast thou done?
I do repent, and yet I do despair,
Hell strives with grace for conquest in my breast:
What shall I do to shun the snares of death?

MEPHOSTOPHILIS

Thou traitor Faustus, I arrest thy soul 65

120

For disobedience to my sovereign lord.
Revolt, or I'll in piecemeal tear thy flesh . . .

[*The two texts coincide for the remainder of the scene, except that
B omits the final appearance (and speech) of the Old Man*]

[Scene 13]

Thunder. Enter LUCIFER, BELZEBUB, *and* MEPHOSTOPHILIS

LUCIFER
    Thus from infernal Dis do we ascend
    To view the subjects of our monarchy,
    Those souls which sin seals the black sons of hell.
    'Mong which as chief, Faustus, we come to thee,
    Bringing with us lasting damnation   5
    To wait upon thy soul; the time is come
    Which makes it forfeit.
MEPHOSTOPHILIS   And this gloomy night,
    Here in this room will wretched Faustus be.
BELZEBUB
    And here we'll stay,
    To mark him how he doth demean himself.   10
MEPHOSTOPHILIS
    How should he, but in desperate lunacy.
    Fond worldling, now his heart-blood dries with grief;
    His conscience kills it, and his labouring brain
    Begets a world of idle fantasies,
    To overreach the devil. But all in vain: 15
    His store of pleasures must be sauced with pain.
    He and his servant Wagner are at hand,
    Both come from drawing Faustus' latest will.
    See where they come.

Enter FAUSTUS *and* WAGNER

FAUSTUS
    Say, Wagner, thou hast perused my will,   20
    How dost thou like it?
WAGNER   Sir, so wondrous well,
    As in all humble duty, I do yield

My life and lasting service for your love.

Enter the SCHOLARS

FAUSTUS
Gramercies Wagner. Welcome gentlemen.
1 SCHOLAR
Now worthy Faustus, methinks your looks are changed.   25
FAUSTUS
O gentlemen!
2 SCHOLAR
What ails Faustus?
FAUSTUS
Ah my sweet chamber-fellow, had I lived with thee,
Then had I lived still, but now must die eternally.
Look sirs, comes he not, comes he not?   30
1 SCHOLAR
O my dear Faustus, what imports this fear?
2 SCHOLAR
Is all our pleasure turned to melancholy?
3 SCHOLAR
He is not well with being over-solitary.
2 SCHOLAR
If it be so, we'll have physicians, and Faustus shall be cured.
3 SCHOLAR
'Tis but a surfeit sir, fear nothing.   35
FAUSTUS
A surfeit of deadly sin, that hath damned both body and soul.
3 SCHOLAR
Yet Faustus, look up to heaven, and remember mercy is infinite.
FAUSTUS
But Faustus' offence can ne'er be pardoned!
The serpent that tempted Eve may be saved,
But not Faustus. O gentlemen, hear with patience, and tremble   40
not at my speeches, though my heart pant and quiver to remem-
ber that I have been a student here these thirty years – O would
I had never seen Wittenberg, never read book; and what wonders
I have done, all Germany can witness – yea, all the world – for
which Faustus hath lost both Germany and the world – yea,   45
heaven itself, heaven, the seat of God, the throne of the blessed,

the kingdom of joy; and must remain in hell for ever. Hell, O hell
for ever. Sweet friends, what shall become of Faustus being in
hell for ever?

2 SCHOLAR

Yet Faustus call on God. 50

FAUSTUS

On God, whom Faustus hath abjured? On God, whom Faustus
hath blasphemed! O my God, I would weep, but the devil draws
in my tears. Gush forth blood instead of tears, yea life and soul:
O, he stays my tongue: I would lift up my hands, but see they hold
'em, they hold 'em. 55

ALL

Who Faustus?

FAUSTUS

Why, Lucifer and Mephostophilis!
O gentlemen, I gave them my soul for my cunning.

ALL

O God forbid.

FAUSTUS

God forbade it indeed, but Faustus hath done it: for the vain 60
pleasure of four-and-twenty years hath Faustus lost eternal joy
and felicity. I writ them a bill with mine own blood, the date is
expired: this is the time, and he will fetch me.

1 SCHOLAR

Why did not Faustus tell us of this before, that divines might have
prayed for thee? 65

FAUSTUS

Oft have I thought to have done so: but the devil threatened to
tear me in pieces if I named God: to fetch me body and soul, if I
once gave ear to divinity: and now 'tis too late. Gentlemen away,
lest you perish with me.

2 SCHOLAR

O what may we do to save Faustus? 70

FAUSTUS

Talk not of me, but save yourselves and depart.

3 SCHOLAR

God will strengthen me; I will stay with Faustus.

1 SCHOLAR

Tempt not God, sweet friend, but let us into the next room, and
pray for him.

FAUSTUS

    Ay, pray for me, pray for me: and what noise soever you hear, come   75
    not unto me, for nothing can rescue me.

2 SCHOLAR

    Pray thou, and we will pray, that God may have mercy upon thee.

FAUSTUS

    Gentlemen farewell. If I live till morning, I'll visit you: if not,
    Faustus is gone to hell.

ALL

    Faustus, farewell.   80

                                  Exeunt SCHOLARS

MEPHOSTOPHILIS

    Ay, Faustus, now thou hast no hope of heaven,
    Therefore despair, think only upon hell;
    For that must be thy mansion, there to dwell.

FAUSTUS

    O thou bewitching fiend, 'twas thy temptation
    Hath robbed me of eternal happiness.   85

MEPHOSTOPHILIS

    I do confess it Faustus, and rejoice!
    'Twas I, that when thou wer't i'the way to heaven,
    Dam'd up thy passage; when thou took'st the book
    To view the Scriptures, then I turned the leaves
    And led thine eye.   90
    What weep'st thou? 'Tis too late; despair; farewell.
    Fools that will laugh on earth, must weep in hell.   *Exit*

        Enter the GOOD ANGEL *and the* BAD ANGEL
                    at several doors

GOOD ANGEL

    O Faustus, if thou hadst given ear to me,
    Innumerable joys had followed thee.
    But thou didst love the world.

BAD ANGEL   Gave ear to me,   95
    And now must taste hell's pains perpetually.

GOOD ANGEL

    O what will all thy riches, pleasures, pomps,
    Avail thee now?

BAD ANGEL   Nothing but vex thee more,
    To want in hell, that had on earth such store.

Music while the throne descends

GOOD ANGEL

O thou has lost celestial happiness,   100
Pleasures unspeakable, bliss without end.
Hadst thou affected sweet divinity,
Hell, or the devil, had had no power on thee.
Hadst thou kept on that way, Faustus behold,
In what resplendent glory thou hadst sat   105
In yonder throne, like those bright shining saints,
And triumphed over hell: that hast thou lost,
And now poor soul must thy good angel leave thee,
The jaws of hell are open to receive thee.   *Exit*

Hell is discovered

BAD ANGEL

Now Faustus, let thine eyes with horror stare   110
Into that vast perpetual torture-house.
There are the Furies tossing damned souls,
On burning forks; there, bodies boil in lead.
There are live quarters broiling on the coals,
That ne'er can die! This ever-burning chair   115
Is for o'er-tortured souls to rest them in.
These, that are fed with sops of flaming fire,
Were gluttons, and loved only delicates,
And laughed to see the poor starve at their gates.
But yet all these are nothing. Thou shalt see   120
Ten thousand tortures that more horrid be.

FAUSTUS

O, I have seen enough to torture me.

BAD ANGEL

Nay, thou must feel them, taste the smart of all.
He that loves pleasure, must for pleasure fall:
And so I leave thee Faustus till anon,   125
Then wilt thou tumble in confusion.

                                                                      Exit

The clock strikes eleven

FAUSTUS

O Faustus,
Now hast thou but one bare hour to live,

And then thou must be damned perpetually.
Stand still, you ever moving spheres of heaven,   130
That time may cease, and midnight never come.
Fair Nature's eye, rise, rise again and make
Perpetual day: or let this hour be but a year,
A month, a week, a natural day,
That Faustus may repent, and save his soul.   135
O lente lente currite noctis equi!
The stars move still, time runs, the clock will strike.
The devil will come, and Faustus must be damned.
O I'll leap up to heaven: who pulls me down?
One drop of blood will save me; O my Christ,   140
Rend not my heart for naming of my Christ.
Yet will I call on him: O spare me Lucifer.
Where is it now? 'Tis gone.
And see a threatening arm, an angry brow.
Mountains and hills, come, come, and fall on me,   145
And hide me from the heavy wrath of heaven.
No? Then will I headlong run into the earth:
Gape earth! O no, it will not harbour me.
You stars that reigned at my nativity,
Whose influence hath allotted death and hell,   150
Now draw up Faustus like a foggy mist,
Into the entrails of yon labouring cloud,
That when you vomit forth into the air,
My limbs may issue from your smoky mouths,
But let my soul mount, and ascend to heaven.   155

The watch strikes

O half the hour is past: 'twill all be past anon!
O, if my soul must suffer for my sin.
Impose some end to my incessant pain!
Let Faustus live in hell a thousand years,
A hundred thousand, and at last be saved.   160
No end is limited to damned souls.
Why wert thou not a creature wanting soul?
Or why is this immortal that thou hast?
O Pythagoras' *metempsychosis* – were that true,
This soul should fly from me, and I be changed   165
Into some brutish beast.

All beasts are happy, for when they die,
Their souls are soon dissolved in elements,
But mine must live still to be plagued in hell.
Cursed be the parents that engendered me;   170
No Faustus, curse thyself, curse Lucifer,
That hath deprived thee of the joys of heaven.

The clock strikes twelve

It strikes, it strikes! Now body, turn to air,
Or Lucifer will bear thee quick to hell.
O soul be changed into small water drops,   175
And fall into the ocean, ne'er be found.

Thunder, and enter the DEVILS

O mercy heaven, look not so fierce on me;
Adders and serpents, let me breathe awhile!
Ugly hell, gape not! Come not Lucifer!
I'll burn my books! O Mephostophilis!   180

                                              Exeunt

[Scene 13b]

*[An additional scene, inserted between Faustus's soliloquy
and the final Chorus]*

Enter the SCHOLARS

1 SCHOLAR
Come gentlemen, let us go visit Faustus,
For such a dreadful night was never seen
Since first the world's creation did begin.
Such fearful shrieks and cries were never heard!
Pray heaven the doctor have escaped the danger.   5

2 SCHOLAR
O help us heaven! See, here are Faustus' limbs,
All torn asunder by the hand of death.

3 SCHOLAR
The devils whom Faustus served have torn him thus!
For 'twixt the hours of twelve and one, methought
I heard hm shriek and call aloud for help: 10

127

At which self time the house seemed all on fire
With dreadful horror of these damned fiends.

2 SCHOLAR

Well gentlemen, tho' Faustus' end be such
As every Christian heart laments to think on,
Yet, for he was a scholar, once admired   15
For wondrous knowledge in our German schools,
We'll give his mangled limbs due burial.
And all the students, clothed in mourning black,
Shall wait upon his heavy funeral.

Exeunt

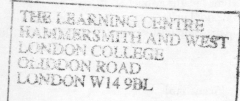